The Coolest People in Comedy: 250 Anecdotes

David Bruce

Published by David Bruce, 2022.

While every precaution has been taken in the preparation of this book, the publisher assumes no responsibility for errors or omissions, or for damages resulting from the use of the information contained herein.

THE COOLEST PEOPLE IN COMEDY: 250 ANECDOTES

First edition. September 13, 2022.

ISBN: 979-8215459362

Written by David Bruce.

Table of Contents

Dedication

DEDICATED TO MY SISTER MARTHA

Martha wrote, "When I was working at Longaberger, I worked with a girl who had two children and was in the middle of a divorce. She was so worried about Christmas for her boys. I received a very nice Christmas bonus that year, and I went to my boss and started a donation fund for the girl. My boss told me later that she — my boss — delivered the money to the girl's mother and father and told them not to tell her who brought the money for her. Months later the girl told me that the boys had the best Christmas that year, and she told me someone had brought money to her mom and dad for her, and she went to town and bought the boys Christmas. She never did know who did that for her. She was so thankful. I believe that I was the only one who donated to her, which was just fine."

***

The doing of good deeds is important. As a free person, you can choose to live your life as a good person or as a bad person. To be a good person, do good deeds. To be a bad person, do bad deeds. If you do good deeds, you will become good. If you do bad deeds, you will become bad. To become the person you want to be, act as if you already are that kind of person. Each of us chooses what kind of person we will become. To become a good person, do the things a good person does. To become a bad person, do the things a bad person does. The opportunity to take action to become the kind of person you want to be is yours.

Bai Juyi went to Zen master Daolin of the Tang Dynasty and asked what one must do in order to live in accord with the Tao. Daolin answered, "One must avoid doing evil, and one must do as much good as possible." Bai Juyi was surprised at the simplicity of this answer and said, "Even a child knows that." "True," replied Daolin, "even a child of three knows this but even a man of 80 fails to live up to it."

A seeker after truth once asked a wise person how to seek God. The wise person replied, "The ways to God are as many as there are created beings. But the shortest and easiest is to serve others, not to bother others, and to make others happy."

The Zen master Gisan was taking a bath. The water was too hot, so he asked a student to add some cold water to the bath. The student brought a bucket of cold water, added some cold water to the bath, and then threw the rest of the water on a rocky path. Gisan scolded the student: "Everything can be used. Why did you waste the rest of the water by pouring it on the path? There are some plants nearby which could have used the water. What right do you have to waste even a drop of water?" The student became enlightened and changed his name to Tekisui, which means "Drop of Water."

"While walking along a river, two monks noticed a lettuce leaf floating downstream. "How sad," said one of the monks, who knew that Zen master Gisan lived one mile upstream. "Gizan has started to waste food." Just then, Gisan burst out of the bushes, panting and sweating, jumped into the river, and began to swim downstream after the lettuce leaf. The two monks bowed low in the direction of Zen master Gisan, then they continued their walk.

Cover Photograph for *The Coolest People in Comedy: 250 Anecdotes:*
Jimmy Durante: Public Domain
https://en.wikipedia.org/wiki/Jimmy_Durante#/media/
File:Jimmy_durante_1964.JP

***

This is a short, quick, and easy read.
Anecdotes are usually short humorous stories. Sometimes they are thought-provoking or informative, not amusing.

***

Educate Yourself
Read Like A Wolf Eats
Be Excellent to Each Other
Books Then, Books Now, Books Forever

***

Do you know a language other than English? If you do, I give you permission to translate this book, copyright your translation, publish or self-publish it, and keep all the royalties for yourself. (Do give me credit, of course, for the original book.)

Chapter 1: From Acting to Christmas

Acting

• Whoopi Goldberg has had excellent success as an actress. When Stephen Spielberg told her that he wanted her to make her film-acting debut in his movie *The Color Purple*, she was happy. In fact, she says, "My teeth caught cold 'cause all I could do was grin." However, she did have to think about appearing in the movie. At first, she thought that Mr. Spielberg wanted her to play a small role, but instead he wanted her to play a major role. But she did not think about it for long. She realized that this was Mr. Spielberg wanting her to be in his movie, so she thought, *Wake up, stupid. Say yes*. She did say yes, and she was nominated for the Best Actress Oscar but did not win. Later, she was nominated for a Best Supporting Actress Oscar for her performance in *Ghost* — and won. In her acceptance speech, she said that she had been practicing making an acceptance speech for an Oscar since she was a little girl, and she joked, "My brother's sitting out there, saying, 'Thank god, we don't have to listen to her anymore.'"[1]

• On *The Drew Carey Show*, Mimi Bobeck, played by Kathy Kinney, became a breakout character and Ms. Kinney became a major co-star, although Mimi was originally conceived as a minor character. Mimi, known for her outrageous makeup and clothing and hatred for all things Drew, owes a lot to Ms. Kinney, who is able to make funny many actions that seem to lack funniness. For example, in one scene, she had to obey the direction, *Mimi hands an envelope to Drew*. But instead of merely handing the envelope to Drew, first Ms. Kinney coughed on it. Ms. Kinney says, "In that moment, Mimi was born."[2]

• Actresses sometimes have love scenes in movies, and some actresses find these scenes difficult to do. Ellen DeGeneres once was asked to do a lesbian love scene with Sharon Stone in an Anne Hecht-directed segment of HBO's *If These Walls Could Talk 2*. Ms. DeGeneres at first did not want to do the scene, but she gave in after

Ms. Hecht pointed out, "I've made out with some weasels [on film], and I got you Sharon Stone!"[3]

• When Chris Rock made the movie *Nurse Betty* with veteran actor Morgan Freeman, he would sometimes overact. Mr. Freeman had an interesting way of showing Mr. Rock that he was overacting: Mr. Freeman would overact, too, and Mr. Rock knew that he had to start acting instead of overacting.[4]

Ad-Libs

• Back when vaudeville was alive and well, Eddie Cantor and George Jessel were performing together. Mr. Cantor made an ad-lib that got a big laugh, and then Mr. Jessel made an ad-lib that got an even bigger laugh. Not knowing anything to say to get a bigger laugh than Mr. Jessel, Mr. Cantor took off a shoe and hit Mr. Jessel on the head with it. Upset, in part because of the huge laugh that Mr. Cantor had gotten by hitting him, Mr. Jessel started complaining to the audience, "Ladies and gentlemen, this so-called grown-up man, whom I have the misfortune to be working with, is so lacking in decorum, breeding, and intelligence, that when he was unable to think of a clever retort he had to descend to the lowest form of humor by taking off his shoe and striking me on the head. Only an insensitive oaf would sink so low." Mr. Cantor had the perfect response to Mr. Jessel's speech. He hit Mr. Jessel on the head with his shoe again.[5]

• Being an insult comedian has its advantages. Comedians Don Rickles and Joan Rivers performed together in Miami, Florida. A Florida judge asked, "Mr. Rickles, why don't you come have lunch and play golf tomorrow?" If he had asked Ms. Rivers, she would have politely replied, "Oh, I'm so sorry. I have a prior family engagement and I can't get out of it, but thank you." Mr. Rickles, on the other hand, is an insult comedian, so he replied, "Listen: One, I'm leaving town. Two, you're a putz. You're loud, obnoxious, incredibly boring, and I wouldn't play golf with you because I don't live here and you couldn't fix a ticket.

No." What was the judge's response to being insulted by a famous insult comedian? He laughed.[6]

• Comedian Joey Bishop was quick with an ad-lib and with a joke. One evening he was performing in a nightclub when glamorous actress Marilyn Monroe came in wearing very expensive furs. Mr. Bishop said to her, "Marilyn, I told you to sit in the truck." And after he got a small part in the movie *The Naked and the Dead*, he told an audience, "I played both parts." Mr. Bishop didn't mind making fun of his good friend Frank Sinatra, who did mind when people other than Mr. Bishop made fun of him. Mr. Bishop once said about his good friend, "Frank regularly calls Dial-A-Prayer to pick up his messages."[7]

• One of stand-up comedian Greg Dean's students made the mistake of rehearsing her act silently instead of out loud, with the result that, as Mr. Dean had predicted, she forgot her act when she got up in front of a nightclub audience. Fortunately, she maintained a playful attitude and got a few laughs ad-libbing a few jokes about forgetting her act. When Mr. Dean yelled out a few words to remind her of the topic of one of her funniest bits, she got a laugh by saying to him, "Thanks, Greg, now I have to stay up here and actually do my show."[8]

• On Jack Benny's radio show, Virgil Reimer, the show's sound-effects man, ran into a problem. A telephone was supposed to ring on the show, and he had just discovered that the machine that was supposed to make the sound of a telephone had weak batteries and wasn't working. Therefore, Mr. Reimer said into a microphone, "Ding-a-ling-ling." The audience in the radio studio laughed, and Mr. Benny ad-libbed, "I'll get it — it sounds like a person-to-person call."[9]

• British comedian Danny La Rue performed in drag, and he was very funny. One night, a woman in the audience was annoyed that her boyfriend was paying attention to Mr. La Rue's performance instead of paying attention to her, so she bared her breasts and told her boyfriend, "Look — these are real." From the stage, Mr. La Rue said, "Yes, darling, they are — but I can hang mine up when it's hot!"[10]

Advertising

• The profit motive makes many retailers feel kindly toward men who like to dress like women. Joan Rivers was selling some of her bejeweled products on the Home Shopping Network when a person named "Margaret" telephoned to rave about a certain bejeweled product she had previously purchased. Based on the sound of Margaret's voice, Miss Veronica Vera, founder of Miss Vera's Finishing School for Boys Who Want to be Girls, wondered whether Margaret's real name might be Pete rather than Peggy. Ms. Rivers didn't care either way — she kept on plugging her bejeweled products.[11]

• A hotel owner once telephoned comedian George Jessel to find out how much he would charge for a performance. When Mr. Jessel said his price was $1,000, the hotel owner offered, "I'll tell you what I'll do for you, Georgie, my boy. I'll give you $500 and put your picture in the Sunday *Times* in my ad." Mr. Jessel replied, "I'll tell you what I'll do for you, Julius, my boy. You give me $1,000 and you can put your picture in the Sunday *Times* in your ad."[12]

Alcohol

• When children's mystery writer Joan Lowery Nixon was young, her parents moved the family to a new house, very close to the house owned by W.C. Fields. Being both observant and curious, Ms. Nixon noticed that a closet in her new home was unusual in that it could be locked from the inside. She investigated, using a measuring tape, and discovered that the closet was in front of another, hidden space. Her mother would not let her investigate further, but after Mr. Fields died, Ms. Nixon toured his house in the presence of a real-estate agent, who showed her a hidden room that had been used to hide liquor during Prohibition. Both houses — that of Mr. Fields and that of Ms. Nixon's family — had been built during Prohibition.[13]

• Some comedians take a drink to steady their nerves before performing. George Gobel once had Garry Moore as a guest on *The George Gobel Show*. Mr. Moore visited Mr. Gobel in his dressing room before the live TV show started, and Mr. Gobel motioned to a bottle of whiskey and said, "Have a drink." However, Mr. Moore replied, "Thanks, but I don't believe I'll have anything before the show. I'll be happy to join you for a drink after the show." Mr. Gobel could hardly believe what he was hearing: "Garry, do you mean to say you go out there *all alone*?"[14]

• Comedian Bill Hicks used to do a lot of drugs, especially alcohol. Fortunately, after going on a late-night drug binge, then doing a radio show at 7 in the morning — during which he was funny although his heart was pounding instead of beating — he decided that he needed help. Mr. Hicks asked a friend who was currently peaceful although he had formerly been wild and crazy, "Are you going to one of those AA meetings today?" The friend replied, "I've been waiting three years for you to say that. There's a meeting in 15 minutes. Let's go."[15]

• While the movie *The Captain Hates the Sea* was being filmed on location, the atmosphere was that of a party, and expenses mounted quickly. Columbia studio head Harry Cohn wired the director, Lewis Milestone: "HURRY UP! THE COST IS STAGGERING!" Mr. Milestone sent back this telegram: "SO IS THE CAST."[16]

• In his home, W.C. Fields kept a chalkboard on which he listed his appointments. When comic writer H. Allen Smith visited him, Mr. Fields had listed, "Stay home and meditate on the follies of humankind. P.S. Get stiff."[17]

Animals

• As a small boy, Wally Cox owned a cat that was smarter than he was and smarter than the adult humans in his household. For example, like all house pets, this cat would sometimes be accidentally shut in a room with all the doors and windows closed. When that happened, the cat would meow, then wait. If that didn't bring a human running to let the cat out of the room, then the cat would knock something small off a shelf or table onto the floor, then wait. If that didn't bring a human running to let the cat out of the room, then the cat would knock something large off a shelf or table onto the floor, then wait. The bigger items made lots of noise, and soon a human would come running to let the cat out of the room. Once the cat was shut in the basement with lots of canning jars. This time, however, the humans thought that they would train the cat. No matter how many jars of canned goods the cat knocked onto the floor, the humans would NOT come running to let the cat out of the basement. The cat knocked a canning jar onto the floor, then another, and then another — until 32 canning jars were on the floor. The humans remained resolute, and did not come running to let the cat out of the basement. Then a truly major racket exploded in the basement, and the humans came running and opened the door to the basement. The cat came out of the basement — objective achieved — and walked haughtily away. This is what had happened. An ironing board was at the top of the basement stairs, and the cat had managed to knock it over so that it crashed down the basement stairs. After that experience, the humans were properly trained. Whenever the cat needed to be let out of a room or the basement, the humans came running — quickly.[18]

• When Margaret Cho was in Tibet, she visited a dog monastery, which she describes as a temple for reincarnated monks — that is, monks who went astray during their human lives and who have come back as dogs. Ms. Cho remembers that the temple is quiet: The dogs do not bark, howl, or fight, and at the temple the major activity of both monks and dogs is quiet meditation. Visitors can feed the dogs pieces of dough, and the dogs wait in line for their turn to eat! Ms. Cho says, "When I think of Tibet, I remember the politeness of the dogs, pulling back their dog lips and ever so gently taking the food from my hand with their open teeth, not wanting to bite my hand accidentally, and then looking warmly into my eyes with a silent thanks."[19]

April Fools Day

• Someone at Google Maps has a sense of humor. Close to April Fools Day, an editor of the website Nevada Thunder asked it for directions from Chicago, Illinois to Amsterdam, Netherlands. Step 20 said, "Swim across the Atlantic Ocean: 3,462 mi."[20]

Audiences

• British comedian David O'Doherty once performed in front of 40 people, 20 of whom were members of the Active Elderly Association, which meant that much of his audience were in their eighties. Unfortunately, his act was not meant for people in their eighties, so he was performing routines about iPhones and about spying on a naked lady doing aerobics when he was 12 years old. During intermission, he figured that all the old people would leave, but they were still present when he walked out for the second half of his act. He asked them, "Why are you still here?" One of the old people replied, "The bus doesn't come to get us until 11." He also used to do readings of children's books in libraries. Ten minutes after he began reading one book, a small boy raised his hand and asked, "Does this get good soon?" Mr. O'Doherty says, "It was so profound. How many times — not just at a gig, but in a relationship or at a family get-together — have you wanted to raise your hand and ask that?"[21]

• Stand-up comedian Kristen Schaal used to practice her act in front of an unusual audience: the cows on the Colorado farm where she grew up. She says, "I had time on my hands. I would perform in front of the cows. They never mooed. They never heckled. They were very polite. That's how I learned to not expect anything from an audience." Despite its being unusual, this kind of audience is good practice for real audiences, as Ms. Schaal points out, "I went back home recently, and I looked at the cows again and thought, 'God, they have the same expression as audiences.' Just expectant — they want something but they're just, like, waiting. And they have no idea what they're waiting for. After that training, I was set."[22]

• Comedian Larry Storch was doing stand-up comedy in Detroit at a time when Soupy Sales was doing a Detroit children's show that was widely watched by adults. Mr. Storch heard that a local TV celebrity was in the audience, and he thought that the audience would like to know that, so he announced, "Ladies and gentlemen, there's a guy named Soupy Sales in the audience who you might know and he's sitting right over there. Let's say hello." Big mistake. The audience mobbed Soupy Sales, leaving nobody to listen to Mr. Storch's act. Mr. Storch says, "It was embarrassing. They left the joint empty."[23]

• Early in his career, British comedian Danny La Rue appeared in a nightclub where the audience sat quietly throughout his performance. He thought that he had bombed completely and that his career was over, until he was informed that previously the audience had always ignored whatever comedian was performing so that they could talk amongst themselves. Getting the audience to listen to his performance was a tremendous achievement, and Mr. La Rue was on his way to a very highly paid career as a comedian.[24]

• Fred Weintraub owned the Bitter End, a club where many comedians plied their art and became famous. He listened to the audience and let its reaction decide whether he should keep an act. If the audience hated an act, he kept it. If the audience loved an act, he kept it. If the audience members said after a performance, "That's a nice act," he dropped that act. According to Mr. Weintraub, the one thing he did not want was for an audience to be indifferent.[25]

• Comedian Eddie Cantor often spoke in Christian churches, and when he was present "officially" for a charity, the church was usually standing room only. But when he dropped in without advance notice, the church would often be half-empty. Once he ended a speech by saying, "Your minister tells me you've set an attendance record today. I suppose I should be honored — but isn't it a shame that God Himself isn't a big enough attraction!"[26]

• Starting out as a stand-up comedian can be tough. Dallas comedian Sherry Belle remembers getting laughs her first time on stage; unfortunately, the audience was laughing at all the wrong places.

For example, she finished a joke, but the audience didn't laugh, so she said, "That was the punch line." That made the audience laugh.[27]

• Sam Mayo was a British music-hall comedian who was popular for a time, but whose comedy fell out of favor and forced his retirement. After retiring, he used to stand outside of music halls listening to the applause given to other performers as tears ran down his cheeks.[28]

Auditions

• Jim J. Bullock is famous in part for playing Monroe Ficus on the TV sitcom *Too Close for Comfort*. To get the part, he first had to perform at the audition, which started late and kept him waiting for an hour. Mr. Bullock stormed into the audition, threw a hissy fit — and threw the screenplay at the feet of the producer — screamed that he should never have been kept waiting that long, and stormed out. A moment later, he entered the room again — on his hands and knees, begging for the job. Everyone laughed, and he got the part.[29]

• Comedian Robin Williams earned great fame as Mork of the TV sitcom *Mork and Mindy*. Mork was an outer-space alien, and when Mr. Williams was asked at an audition to sit in a chair while in character as Mork, he did exactly that — and sat on his head. Fame really did come quickly. At an ice-skating rink, Mr. Williams stepped into a telephone booth to make a call. He was recognized by fans, who gawked at him through the glass. Mr. Williams says, "I felt like I was in the San Diego Zoo."[30]

Autographs

• Morris "Moe" Feinberg was the brother of Larry Fine, one of the Three Stooges. Mr. Feinberg went to a nightclub in Atlantic City, where an entertainer recognized him and introduced him to the audience, talking about the Three Stooges and saying, "I see Larry's brother, Moe Fine, a good friend and a fellow performer. Moe, would you stand up and take a bow?" Afterward, a woman came up and asked for Mr. Feinberg's autograph. He explained that he was only a small-time performer and not famous, but the woman smiled and said, "You can't fool me with that 'brother' stuff. You're Larry, all right." Mr. Feinberg signed the autograph, "With warm regards, Larry 'Stooge' Fine."[31]

• English comedian Benny Hill appears to have been very likeable in real life. For one thing, he answered every letter from fans and never turned down a request for an autographed photograph. Also making him popular, of course, was his talent at being funny. Mr. Hill did joke about his public image as a comic lover. He used to say, "I imagine people also think I'm having it off with the girls in my show. Well, I haven't had it off with them since ... what time is it now?" and "This is the book where I keep the names of all the girls I've been to bed with. They're in alphabetical order. Starting with Zelda."[32]

• Being a popular entertainer does have drawbacks. Country comedian Jerry Clower once ordered a ham dinner at Cracker Barrel, but he never did eat it because his gravy got cold as he signed 39 menus. He ended up going to a Seven-Eleven and buying crackers and Vienna sausages.[33]

• Groucho Marx wrote this note in reply to an 11-year-old autograph collector: "Here is the autograph. I would send you a lock of my hair but it's at the barbershop getting washed."[34]

Automobiles

• When he was a teenager, Soupy Sales used to double-date with a friend named Bill Cravens. The two would take their dates to a movie, go to the park to neck (smooch) for a while, and then get something to eat. On one double-date, Soupy's date didn't want to go to the park because she said she wasn't feeling well, so Soupy told Bill that they needed to take his date home. She asked, "Aren't we going to get something to eat?" Soupy replied, "If you're too sick to neck, you're too sick to eat." Back when Soupy was a teenager, not every teenager who was old enough to drive had a car. On his double-dates, a friend with a car would drop Soupy off at his date's friend's house, and then the friend with a car would pick up his date and then come back to get Soupy and his date. Once, Soupy was in a house waiting for his date to come down from upstairs. The young woman's father said, "Gee, I wonder what's keeping Elaine?" Soupy said, "Wait a minute! Isn't this Joanne Pinckard's house? The young woman's father said, "No, Joanne lives across the street."[35]

Beauty

• In 2008, comedian Margaret Cho debuted a new show: *Beautiful.* The genesis of the show came when a radio host asked Ms. Cho, "What would you do if you woke up tomorrow and you were beautiful?" She was shocked by the question because, as people who know and love her (or see her) realize, she *is* beautiful. She asked the radio host, "What?" and he explained, "What if you woke up and you were blond, blue-eyed, 5' 11" and weighed 100 lbs and you were beautiful, what would you do?" Uh — 5' 11" and 100 lbs! Ms. Cho says, "I told him I probably wouldn't get up because I would be too weak to stand!" She also thought, "It upset me because I thought if that was the only person he thinks is beautiful, he must not see much beauty ever. I wanted to do a show about how we are all beautiful. It is something I have to constantly tell myself."[36]

• Apparently, the Ziegfeld Follies' Flo Ziegfeld was a good judge of feminine beauty but lacked a sense of humor. He once watched W.C. Fields make the audience roar with laughter with a comedy sketch, then asked how long the sketch had taken. The answer came back: 28 minutes. Mr. Ziegfeld next asked how long it took for the girls to get ready for the next scene. The answer came back: seven minutes. Mr. Ziegfeld then ordered Mr. Fields to cut his comedy sketch to seven minutes.[37]

Children

• As a small boy, Wally Cox learned that some of the best things in life could be purchased with a box top from a box of cereal or the aluminum seal from a jar of Ovaltine. Just send in a box top or an aluminum seal and a small amount of money to cover shipping and handling, and all kinds of neat stuff — including a Cub reporter's certificate (from a radio program starring Dick Steel, the boy reporter) — would arrive in your mailbox. The aluminum seal from a jar of Ovaltine bought young Wally the knowledge of how to decode the secret messages that were broadcast at the end of the Little Orphan Annie radio program — secret messages that gave hints about Little Orphan Annie's next exciting adventure. Young Wally was proud to know the code: A is 2, B is 4, C is 6, etc. Unfortunately, soon after young Wally learned how to decode the secret messages, the dullest boy in school told him, "Hey, you wanna know the Little Orphan Annie secret code? A is 2, B is 4, C is 6 ...." Disappointed at being unable to amaze even the dullest boy in school with his foreknowledge of Little Orphan Annie's next exciting adventure, young Wally soon stopped sending away for things that required payment of a box top or an aluminum seal.[38]

• Some people are fortunate in that they know what they want to do at an early age. When she was six, lesbian comedian Liz Feldman saw a Purim play at her synagogue in which her 11-year-old sister played Queen Esther. After the show, Liz pointed to the stage and told her mother, "That's what I want to do!" At age 10, she asked her parents for an agent for her birthday. Unfortunately, she got a 10-speed bicycle instead. At age 12, she started auditioning in Manhattan. At age 15, she answered an ad looking for children who wrote and performed their own stand-up material, so she wrote three minutes of material and got a role in a play about very young stand-up comedians. One of the jokes she wrote — which she now considers "so bad" and yet "so gay" — is this: "You know how some kids will get embarrassed when their moms will spit on a napkin to wipe the dirt off their face? My mom just licks my face."[39]

• Jim Carrey was funny even as a youngster. One of his "acts" was to put a lot of colored candies in his mouth, chew them up, and then pretend to vomit. His very young audience loved it. In school, he once got in trouble when his teacher saw him mocking some musicians on a record. Fortunately, all turned out well. Thinking to embarrass him, his teacher ordered him to do what he was doing in front of the class. Young Jim did, and he was so funny that his teacher invited him to do the act at the school's Christmas assembly. And when his mother became ill, Jim's comedy cheered her up — sometimes at odd times. Occasionally, his father would wake him up and say, "Sorry to wake you up in the middle of the night, but your mother and I could use a good laugh. You're on in five."[40]

• As you may expect, comedian George Carlin took too many illegal drugs in his life. According to journalist David Hochman, when Mr. Carlin and his 11-year-old daughter took a vacation to Hawaii, she made him sign a contract stating that he wouldn't snort cocaine for the duration of the vacation. Despite his illegal drug use, and despite his heart problems, he got old, something that really wasn't a problem for him. He stated that "the richness of memory, the richness of acquired and accumulated experience and wisdom, I won't trade that. At 67, I'm every age I ever was. I always think of that. I'm not just 67. I'm also 55 and 21 and three. Oh, especially three."[41]

• David Letterman was an original even in high school. For an English assignment he was required to write about an important event in a person's life, so he wrote about a man who had swallowed paper towels — his way of committing suicide. While working at a grocery store, David once put cornhusks in a box of cornflakes and put it on the shelf. Not everyone was impressed by him — or his sense of humor. His high-school guidance counselor, Marilyn Dearing, wrote that he was "a run-of-the-mill ordinary average kid." In an interview after he became famous, she said, "I didn't think David was funny then, and I still don't think he is funny."[42]

• George Burns was Jewish, but once he wanted to become Presbyterian. Why? As a small child, he was a member of a singing group that sang in an amateur talent contest at a church picnic. They won first prize — each boy received a watch. Young George was so excited that he ran home and told his mother that he wanted to become a Presbyterian — he had been a Jew all seven years of his life and never gotten anything, and he had been a Presbyterian for 15 minutes and gotten a watch. His mother told him, "First help me hang up the wash, then you can be a Presbyterian."[43]

• Frank Sinatra loved his kids. Sometimes, he took daughter Tina out to eat. She was surprised that so many people stared at her in restaurants. Frank was embarrassed as he said to her, "They're not staring at you, Pigeon. They're staring at me." Frank's love for Tina worked out well for television comedian Soupy Sales, who was happy to get a telephone call one day from a major, major star: "I'm Frank Sinatra. My kid wants me to do your show."[44]

• Like father, like son. When comedian Robin Williams was a boy, he had a large collection of various kinds of toy soldiers, and he would engage the soldiers in time-machine battles. For example, he would pit World War II soldiers with machine guns against knights in shining armor. Zach, Robin's son, is also original. At his first formal-wear event, he didn't wear a tuxedo — he wore camouflage and Doc Martin boots.[45]

• As a boy, Quaker humorist Tom Mullen attended Boys' State, where a military officer inspected him and some other lads. Young Tom had some fuzz on his cheeks, so the officer asked, "What's the matter, son? Don't you have a razor?" Young Tom replied, "Yes, sir, but I don't lend it to strangers." The witticism drew laughs from the other boys — and the largest number of demerits possible from the officer.[46]

• Ron Howard, of course, was only five years old when he started co-starring in *The Andy Griffith Show*. Later, he became a renowned Hollywood director. Comedian George Lindsey, who played Goober, was once asked what he thought of his little co-star Ronny's work as a director. He replied, "We call him Mr. Howard now."[47]

• The early life of comedian Bill Cosby was not one of privilege. One place he lived in as a child lacked a bathtub, so the Cosby children would put a metal tub on the stove to heat the water, then move the tub to the floor and take a bath.[48]

Christmas

• When Fanny Brice's husband, Nicky Arnstein, went to jail, Fanny kept the truth from their children, telling them that their father was working in Paris. For Christmas, the children wrote their father, telling him that they wanted a pair of rabbits for Christmas. Fanny therefore arranged to have two rabbits shipped from Paris to their home, along with lots of food and water to keep the rabbits healthy. However, when the crate was opened in the United States, many more than two rabbits hopped out — the journey had been long, and the rabbits had been doing what rabbits do. The children thought that their father had been especially generous that Christmas.[49]

• One Christmas, comedian W.C. Fields called a locksmith to come to his house on an emergency. When the locksmith arrived, Mr. Field showed him a door with a lock in which a key had been broken. "My best friend is trapped in there!" Mr. Fields cried. "Do something before he smothers to death!" However, when the locksmith opened the door, nothing was to be found except many, many bottles of liquor.[50]

• Early in his career, stand-up comedian Greg Dean made little money and consequently had no money to buy Christmas presents. Therefore, he developed a comedy routine, then went to the houses of his friends and relatives, where he gave the routine and made that their Christmas present.[51]

Chapter 2: From Clothing to Football

Clothing

• Comedian Fannie Brice needed time to develop a sense of fashion. When Ziegfeld Follies impresario Florenz "Flo" Ziegfeld invited her and Lillian Lorraine to dinner, Fannie went all out in acquiring what she thought was an outfit that would impress Mr. Ziegfeld. Among other items, she bought a hat that looked as if it was growing a vegetable garden. Unfortunately, her outfit horrified Mr. Ziegfeld, who was a man of taste. He told Ms. Lorraine, a woman of taste, "Why don't you take this kid out and teach her how to dress? Here is $250. Get her some clothes." Ms. Brice did not throw her hat away, but instead she sold it to Ms. Lorraine's maid. Unfortunately for Mr. Ziegfeld, the maid wore the hat one day while traveling with Ms. Lorraine. Mr. Ziegfeld saw the hat, and he was so upset that he told the maid, "I never want to see that hat again. I'll give you $25 [a lot of money in the early 20th century] to get rid of it."[52]

• Early in their careers, British comedians Dawn French and Jennifer Saunders shared a house. Ms. Saunders was known for being disorganized and messy, although she later became much neater after having children. Unfortunately, their house was broken into. They called the police, who investigated and said, "Well, it is quite bad, but the worst is that room at the top." Actually, the burglars hadn't entered the room at the top. That room was Ms. Saunders' room, and it was in its usual messy state. Ms. French says about Ms. Saunders, "She used to be up to her knees in old pants."[53]

• Groucho Marx once knew a comedian named Doc Rockwell who took an odd approach to saving money. He used to buy several new suits at one time to get a discount, then he would wear a suit for a month, throw it away, and wear one of his other suits for a month, repeating the process until he ran out of suits. He would then buy several new suits at a discount and start the process again. He once explained to Groucho, "This way, I don't have to pay for any cleaning and pressing and, besides, I'm always wearing a brand-new suit."[54]

• Caroline Otéro and Liane de Pougy were members of the 19th-century French glitterati. Their rivalry was on display at a great ball they were both invited to attend in Paris. Ms. Otéro arrived wearing a beautiful black dress and every piece of jewelry she owned. Arriving a few minutes later was Ms. de Pougy, who wore the same style of dress — but in white — and no jewelry. Trailing Ms. de Pougy was her maid — who was wearing every piece of jewelry that Ms. de Pougy owned.[55]

• The first time country music star Bill Anderson saw country comedian Jerry Clower, he got mad at him because Mr. Clower was wearing exactly the same kind of coat that he was wearing. Mr. Anderson thought, "How dare him to have a coat exactly like mine!" Fortunately, Mr. Clower's reaction kept Mr. Anderson from staying mad at him. Mr. Clower said, "You mean I got the good taste to buy a coat exactly like the [coat of the] great Bill Anderson?"[56]

• In 1924, the Prince of Wales visited Fanny Brice's apartment in New York. She told him, "Sit down, kid, and take off your shoes. While you're relaxing, I'll whip up a couple of smoked sturgeon sandwiches on rye with some marvelous pickles a guy on Delancey Street puts up for me." The Prince of Wales told her, "Miss Brice, I thank you from the bottom of my heart," then he took off his shoes.[57]

• Comedians George Burns and Harpo Marx were members of the Hillcrest Country Club in Beverly Hills, as so many Jewish comedians were. Unfortunately, the Hillcrest Country Club once briefly considered kicking them out. Why? On an especially hot day, the two comedians had played a round of golf wearing only their underwear.[58]

• Sharon Linkletter, Art's daughter, made a lot of her own clothing. Once she made a bikini from a pattern, then showed the bottom of the bikini to her mother. Her mother asked, "Where are you going to wear that?" Sharon said, "On the bottom, of course." Her mother replied, "I mean — are you going to wear that in public?"[59]

Competition

• W.C. Fields was so competitive that watching movies by other good comedians made him ill. He once started to watch a movie by Charlie Chaplin, but he grew so ill that he had to leave the movie theater. When he was asked his opinion of Mr. Chaplin, Mr. Fields snarled, "The son of a bitch is a ballet dancer — and if I get a good chance, I'll kill him with my bare hands."[60]

• Comedian Sid Caesar, star of *Your Show of Shows*, was good — very good. How good was he? While fellow comedian Robin Williams was watching some of the old episodes of *Your Show of Shows*, a woman who was also in the audience told him, "You'll never be that good."[61]

Critics

• A bad review can give birth to a good joke. David Woods and Jon Haynes make up the anarchic theatrical group known as Ridiculusmus, although it used to have more members. In 1993, critic John O'Mahony was very impressed with Mr. Woods, and he wrote about him, "He transforms every bit-part into a central character, while showing up the paucity of talent in the rest of the group." For years after the review appeared, whenever Mr. O'Mahony saw the group, Mr. Woods would be genial — but nervous — and the other members of the group would glower at Mr. O'Mahony and hiss at him. By the way, the group now consists of just two people, but that has nothing to do with Mr. O'Mahony's review. The two remaining members do work well together. Mr. Woods says, "I think we complement each other." Mr. Haynes adds, "Some like his exuberance. Others prefer my intensity. And a lot don't like either of us." At the very beginning of their careers, they had a comedy venue called the Tomato Club. They invited bad comedians to perform, and they gave audience members overripe tomatoes to throw at the bad comedians. With good reason, Mr. Haynes is concerned about critical notices: "Critical success would upset our equilibrium. Who can we bribe at the [British newspaper] *Guardian* to give us a one-star review?"[62]

• Elaine May went backstage to see Dudley Moore after a Broadway performance of Beyond the Fringe and told him, "I loved the show." When Mr. Moore, who was in a mood for receiving lots of reassurance, asked her if she had really loved the show, Ms. May, who was not in a mood for giving lots of reassurance, replied, "No."[63]

Death

• British comedian Stephen Mangan started out studying law, then switched to serious acting, and finally started performing comic roles. He read many, many biographies of theatrical actors such as Ellen Terry, John Gielgud, Laurence Olivier, Henry Irving, etc., and he says, "As a 16-year-old, all I wanted was to be living in digs in Darlington, heading off to do the matinee of Charley's Aunt." But he instead studied law, although at school he was around many, many "people who flipped their capes over their shoulders and said, 'I'm going to become an actor.'" Still, when he graduated, he was too afraid to take a chance on theater, and he says that it seemed that he would become "a disgruntled lawyer, a slightly bitter bloke with the world's largest theatrical biography collection." However, his mother died from cancer at age 45, and Mr. Mangan's priorities immediately changed. "From that moment, I heard the clock ticking," he says. "You think, God, if that's how long I've got, why not try and do it?" He tried it, and he succeeded at it.[64]

• Comedian Jerry Seinfeld says, "The honest truth is, for a comedian, even death is just a premise to make jokes about." For example, Mr. Seinfeld telephoned fellow comedian George Carlin a few days before Mr. Carlin died of a heart attack. And of course, Mr. Carlin made jokes about death. Journalist Tim Russert and musician Bo Diddley had recently died, and Mr. Carlin said, "I feel safe for a while. There will probably be a break before they come after the next one. I always like to fly on an airline right after they've had a crash. It improves your odds."[65]

• Groucho Marx got a lot of letters in his old age, but he reasoned that he got so many letters because two of his famous comedian brothers, Chico and Harpo, had died before he did. If they had lived, they would have received many of the letters. Groucho was a skeptic concerning the afterlife. Before Chico and Harpo died, they made a promise to Groucho, who explained, "They said they'd get in touch with me if there were a hereafter." So what happened? Chico died in 1961, Harpo died in 1964, and in an interview with movie critic Roger Ebert in 1970, Groucho said, "I never heard a word. Not a godd*mn word."[66]

Easter

• Bob Ferguson owned a shoe-repair shop in Akron, Ohio, and his shop was notable for its window displays. When a friend suggested that he put a bunny in the window for Easter, Mr. Ferguson displayed a mannequin dressed (undressed?) as a Playboy Bunny.[67]

Education

• Comedian Buster Keaton spent exactly one day in school. At age six, he was already a veteran comedian in vaudeville, thanks to his vaudevillian parents, and he treated school simply as another stage on which to make other people laugh. After disrupting the taking of attendance, the teaching of geography, and the teaching of grammar, he was sent to the principal, who sent Buster back home to his parents with a note pleading with them to keep Buster at home. His parents thought the note was funny, and his mother started teaching Buster at home (and on the road, since they continued their vaudeville act).[68]

• Comedians Jimmy Durante and Don Knotts once co-hosted a *Kraft Music Hall* special on TV. During rehearsal, the director said that when they were introduced, he wanted both of them to walk onstage doing the famous Jimmy Durante strut. In other words, Mr. Durante was supposed to be himself and Mr. Knotts was supposed to imitate

Mr. Durante. However, Mr. Durante was forced to ask Mr. Knotts to show him the famous Jimmy Durante strut. He requested, "Hey, Don, do me! I don't know what I do!"[69]

• One way that comedian Bill Cosby helped schools was through non-intrusive kinds of advertising. On *The Cosby Show*, his character, Cliff Huxtable, frequently wore a sweatshirt that bore the name of a predominantly black college. By the way, when Mr. Cosby hosted *You Bet Your Life*, the duck that dropped down when a contestant said the secret word wore a sweatshirt bearing the name of the university that Mr. Cosby had attended: Temple.[70]

• Comedian Richard Pryor had an understanding teacher named Miss Marguerite Yingst when he was in the 6th grade. He often came to school late, and she made a deal with him. If he came to school on time each day for a week, she would let him get in front of the class and perform for 10 minutes Friday afternoon. She remembers, "It was great for Richard. The other pupils loved him. And Richard kept his promise — got to school on time."[71]

• Garry Moore and Jimmy Durante worked together in radio. They were both comedians, and Mr. Moore was Mr. Durante's chief writer. For one show, Mr. Moore wrote a malapropism for Mr. Durante: "It's a catastastrope!" He also told Mr. Durante, "You know, Jimmy, if you don't mispronounce this, we won't get a laugh." Mr. Durante thought for a moment, then replied, "Yeah. Educate me, and we'll both be out of a job."[72]

• A young Dick Van Dyke and the other students in his class sometimes took advantage of one of their teachers who was hard of hearing. Sometimes, she asked, "When did Columbus discover America?" They would reply with a deliberately wrong date such as "1776" because she would think that they had given the correct date and nod her head approvingly.[73]

• Comedian Chris Rock has made it big in the risky and difficult business of show business, but that doesn't mean that he wants his relatives to try to accomplish what he has accomplished. Whenever a family member wants help in getting established in show business, he offers to pay their college tuition instead.[74]

• The first book Sam Levenson ever checked out of the library shocked the librarians — it was called *What Every Girl Should Know*. (Sam's cousin Sophie was too embarrassed to check it out, so she asked Sam to check it out for her to read.)[75]

Fame

• After movie shorts made by the Three Stooges — Moe, Larry, and Curly — started being shown on TV, the Three Stooges made many, many fans among the kids who saw them on TV. One day, Moe's daughter asked him to pick up his grandchildren — Mike and Jeff — from school. Moe agreed, and when school let out, here came Mike and Jeff — and a couple of hundred other kids. Mike and Jeff had told their friends that one of the Three Stooges was coming to pick them up, and their friends had told their friends, who had told their friends. Things were chaotic for a while, and finally a teacher asked Moe to leave because of the near-riot conditions. By the way, Moe once received a telephone call from his daughter, who told him good news. She had bought a copy of the *World Book Encyclopedia*, and a photograph of the Three Stooges was in it! Later, Moe looked up "Comedy" in the *World Book Encyclopedia*, and he saw a photograph of himself and Larry wrapping an "iron" bar around the neck of Curly.[76]

• In 1959, Mel Brooks, before he became really famous, attended a wrap party at a restaurant for the movie *Happy Anniversary*, in which his friend Carl Reiner appeared. Also eating at the restaurant, across the room, was playwright Moss Hart, whom Mr. Brooks recognized. Mr. Brooks approached Mr. Hart, loudly saying, "Hello. You don't know who I am. My name is Mel Brooks. Do you know who you are? Your name is Moss Hart. Do you know what you've written? You wrote *Once in a Lifetime* with George Kaufman and *You Can't Take It with You* and *The Man Who Came to Dinner*. You wrote *Lady in the Dark* and you directed *My Fair Lady*." Mr. Brooks continued naming all the things that Mr. Hart had accomplished during his life. Then he grew louder, "You should be arrogant! You have earned the right to be supercilious! *WHY* ARE YOU LETTING *ME* TALK TO *YOU*?"[77]

• Charlie Chaplin was widely imitated. One day, he was watching one of his imitators on a street in New York when a small boy pushed him. Mr. Chaplin asked him, "What's the matter?" The small boy said, "Oh, git outa me way. I wanta see Charlie Chaplin. Whada you care about seein' him? Youse guys always gets in a kid's way." On another occasion, Mr. Chaplin had finished shooting a scene in an alley. The people he was working with left, but Mr. Chaplin stayed because he wanted to watch some crap-shooting newsboys. A police officer came by and wanted to run Mr. Chaplin off, but Mr. Chaplin protested, "I'm Charlie Chaplin, and I've been working here!" The police officer replied, "You Charlie Chaplin! Huh, I guess I know Charlie Chaplin when I see him. You're just one of his bum imitators. Get out!"[78]

• As a young comedian, Jim Carrey made out a $10 million check to himself "for acting services rendered," and carried it around in his wallet as a physical symbol of an important goal. Later, he received $10 million for starring in *The Mask 2* — and $20 million for starring in *Liar, Liar*. Along the way to mega-success, he achieved success as an actor in the TV comedy series *In Living Color*. Unfortunately, his fame did have a downside when he took his daughter out for trick-or-treating on Halloween. Perhaps exaggerating a little, Mr. Carrey says that people would say, "It's the dude from *In Living Color*! Here's an extra candy! Do something [funny]!"[79]

• Terry Gilliam considers himself fortunate because he is the least recognized of the members of Monty Python's Flying Circus. He is recognized just enough to keep his ego happy, but he realizes how much of a hassle it would be to be recognized everywhere he went. He says, "Thank God I'm not John. It's an awful job to walk down the street and be John Cleese because you can't escape from it!"[80]

• Stan Laurel was funny in his old age. At a stationery store, a man kind of recognized him, saying, "Aren't you...," but the man was unable to come up with a name, so Mr. Laurel suggested a name: "Oliver Hardy." The man replied, "Right. Whatever happened to Laurel?" Mr. Laurel sadly replied, "Oh, he went balmy."[81]

Fans

• Comedians are often writers; for example, Bill Cosby does much writing — both of comic routines and of books. His old comic routines still hold up. One day, some parents brought their nine-year-old son to see Mr. Cosby. The son was a fan, and he started doing Mr. Cosby's 1966 routine "The Playground." In the routine Bill and his friends play safely in a vacant lot despite the presence of broken glass — but they are no longer safe after someone installs monkey bars. The nine-year-old boy recited the routine, using Mr. Cosby's inflections, and Mr. Cosby says that he started "listening to, and admiring, my writing. The kid's performing, and I'm saying to myself, 'This is really wonderful writing.'"[82]

• Comedian Fred Allen was generous with his time. Whenever a fan wrote him, the fan received a personal reply from the great comedian himself. In addition, Mr. Allen did not repeat himself. If 10 requests for autographs came in the mail, Mr. Allen sent back 10 different replies and not one reply copied 10 times. One of his writers, Arnold M. Auerbach, once asked him why he spent so much time answering fan mail. Mr. Allen replied, "Anyone who takes the time to write to me deserves a personal answer."[83]

• At the premiere of stand-up comedian Sarah Silverman's movie titled *Sarah Silverman: Jesus is Magic*, which includes music in addition to comedy, an enthusiastic fan told her that she was "the true heir to Lenny Bruce." She smiled and replied, "Wow! Thank you! That is the ultimate compliment! I'm actually not that familiar with Lenny Bruce's work, but from what I understand, he was a really great singer."[84]

• Jack Riley played the character of the insulting, misanthropic Mr. Elliott Carlin on *The Bob Newhart Show*. Frequently, fans of the showed asked him if he was anything like the character he portrayed. Because he was a professional comedian, Mr. Riley's standard response to this question was in the character of Mr. Carlin: "Bite me, you wiener."[85]

• Comedian Fred Allen once met a fan who told him that she had traveled to New York all the way from San Francisco to see him broadcast his radio program. Mr. Allen replied, "Madame, if I had only known you were coming all that way just to catch my little old show, the least I could have done was meet you halfway — say, about Omaha."[86]

• A boy named Bobby once wrote a fan letter to comedian Tim Conway and told him to drop by if he was ever in St. Louis, Missouri. The following week, Mr. Conway showed up at Bobby's front door with his suitcase and said, "Hi, Bobby. You told me to drop in anytime, so I thought I'd stay for a week or two."[87]

• When comedian Eddie Cantor performed at Carnegie Hall, a very old man told him, "Mr. Cantor, I've been a fan of yours since I was a little kid." Skeptical, the 60-year-old Mr. Cantor asked the very old man, "And how old are you?" The very old man said, "Ninety."[88]

• Sometimes people go up to celebrities and say, "Your face looks familiar. Haven't I seen it somewhere?" Comedian George Gobel used to reply, "No, it's always been right where it is now."[89]

Fathers

• When Adam Sandler was a little boy, he had a Diver Dan doll. Unfortunately, he lost it. Fortunately, he had a father who cared about him and didn't want him to be unhappy. His father dressed up as Diver Dan's father, then told young Adam that Diver Dan was not lost but instead was with him, and he thanked young Adam for taking care of Diver Dan. Today, Mr. Sandler says, "Dad would do anything to make me feel better."[90]

• When Sarah Silverman was three years old, her father taught her some dirty words, and then he told her to say them to his friends. She and the dirty words got a big laugh. As a grown-up stand-up comedian, Ms. Silverman says, "I realize now the laugh was pure shock value, but it felt really good, and I've been chasing it ever since."[91]

• When Chris Rock was still early in his career as a stand-up comedian, his father asked him how good he was. Chris replied, "I'm one of the best in the country." His father knew him well, and he knew that Chris was not lying.[92]

Food

• As a struggling, impoverished comedian early in his career, Jackie Gleason and some comedian friends found ways to survive. One thing that they would do was to go to a café and order a meal that one of them paid for. Whoever paid for the meal got the entrée. The others ate the potato, the salad, and the dessert, if there was one. They also went to the Automat, got hot water for free, then added packets of ketchup, Tabasco sauce, A-1 steak sauce, and salt and pepper to create something that resembled tomato soup. In addition, they sometimes ate the rolls or bread that a diner left behind. Another trick was to sleep through breakfast. When you're sleeping, you're not hungry. Even later, during his first marriage, things were bad. One February day in 1937, Mr. Gleason got hold of several brochures advertising a one-cent sale. As an advertising gimmick, each brochure had a penny glued to it. Mr. Gleason tore off all the pennies so that he and his wife could buy sandwiches.[93]

• Once in a while, William M. Gaines, publisher of MAD magazine, would invite all the artists and writers to a dinner in a fancy restaurant. (This was a very good idea, as it allowed people — many of them freelancers who just stopped by once in a while to drop off material — to get to know each other. Because the MAD magazine employees were so numerous, they would ask the waiters if they could push some of the tables together. Once given permission, they would quickly form a circle of tables around the waiters, leaving no exit.[94]

• Early in her career — basically before she had a career and while she was still a housewife — Phyllis Diller did a show at the Alameda Naval Air Station, where she was a hit and for which her pay was a 30-pound live turkey. She left it tied outside her apartment that night, and the next morning a couple who lived near her made her an offer: "We're farm people, so we'll kill it and share it with you." Ms. Diller accepted the offer, and each family got 15 pounds of turkey.[95]

• Who was the first comedian to throw a pie in a silent-movie comedy? Probably it was Mabel Normand. In 1913, some of Mack Sennett's comedians, including Mabel and Roscoe "Fatty" Arbuckle, were making a movie, but none of their gags seemed to work. Bored, Mabel saw a pie. Mr. Sennett's comedians, including Mabel, played many practical jokes, and she launched the pie at Fatty Arbuckle, scoring a direct hit and many laughs.[96]

• When comedian Steve Allen was a teenager, he ran away from home. Very quickly, he began to steal, to beg, and to eat garbage. Mr. Allen writes about finding a discarded can of pork and beans along a road. The can contained several ants and a few beans, but Mr. Allen shook the ants out of the can and enjoyed eating what was left of the beans.[97]

• Tommy Morgan was a Scottish comedian. While staying in a Belfast hotel and hosting some friends in the hotel restaurant, Mr. Morgan was treated like the celebrity he was, and a waiter asked, "Will you be having a bit of partridge, Mr. Morgan?" Mr. Morgan replied, "A bit! What do you mean — a bit! Bring us a whole one each."[98]

Football

• When Bill Cosby was in school, his grandfather advised him not to play football. Bill played football anyway, and he broke his shoulder. He was lying on a sofa, in pain, when his grandfather visited. Embarrassed, young Bill waited for his grandfather to say, "See, I told you, Junior." Instead, his grandfather gave him a quarter and told him, "Go to the corner [store] and get some ice cream. It has calcium in it.'"[99]

• Comedian Frank Morgan said whatever was on his mind. Once, he was reading the scores of some obscure football games on his radio program when he suddenly interrupted himself and asked, "Is anybody really interested in this nonsense?"[100]

Chapter 3: From Friends to Mishaps

Friends

• At Friars Club dinners, comedians take great pleasure in insulting the guest of honor, often using very vulgar language to do so. At a dinner for Jack Benny, many dignified people, including Eleanor Roosevelt, Helen Hayes, and Senator Jacob Javits, were present, so Mr. Benny told his friend and fellow comedian George Burns, "George, this is a high-class affair, so nothing risqué." Mr. Burns joked, "Should I tell the story about Sid Gary's *ss?" Mr. Benny joked back, "I wouldn't if I were you, because Javits is on ahead of you, and he's going to tell it."[101]

• Actor Elliott Gould was friends with comedian Groucho Marx when Groucho was old. Groucho, of course, insulted friends as well as enemies. Once, Mr. Gould replaced a burned-out light bulb over Groucho's bed, and Groucho told him, "That's the best acting I've ever seen you do." Mr. Elliott considers that "the best review I've ever had and probably will ever have." The two men really were close — Groucho even let Mr. Elliott shave him with an electric razor.[102]

Gambling

• Even good people can be distracted from what is really important. At one time, comedian Phil Silvers was accustomed to bet quite a lot of money on sports games. Once, he visited with his mother for a day, and he had her radio tuned to a game he had bet on. At the end of the day, he realized that he had spent the day with his mother, but he couldn't remember a single thing she had said because he had been listening to the game, not to her.[103]

• Chico Marx loved to gamble, and he gambled all of his money away. His famous brother Harpo, however, managed to save much of his earnings. Once, Chico was asked how much money he had lost gambling. He replied, "Find out how much Harpo has. That's how much I've lost!"[104]

Gays and Lesbians

• Jennie McNulty is both an out comedian and a defensive back for the California Quake women's football team. She performs at military bases in Iraq and on Olivia cruises for lesbians and at other gay-friendly venues. While performing on military bases, she couldn't delve deeply into gay matters when the military had a "don't ask, don't tell" policy, but she found a way to make a point: "I love doing the military shows. I have to do what I call 'don't ask, don't tell' shows, so I just don't bring up anything relationship-wise, but I'm decked out in rainbow gear from head to toe — Richard Simmons would look straighter than I do performing there." Fortunately, she comes back to gay-friendly venues, so she says that she goes "from 'don't ask' to 'tell everybody'!" She loves the Olivia cruises because of all the lesbians who are free to be themselves. Of course, in the big cities gays and lesbians can be out and about, but in small towns, doing that can be much harder. Ms. McNulty says, "On the Olivia trips, you're dealing with people who live in the middle of the country. I had one woman tell me she and her girlfriend had to practice holding hands, because they can never hold hands when they're home. Those crowds are so amazing because everyone's just on cloud nine — they're totally free to be who they are."[105]

• On April 30, 1997, Ellen DeGeneres' character, Ellen Morgan, came out in the one-hour episode of *Ellen* titled "The Puppy Episode." The title of the episode was an in-joke: At a meeting to get ideas for episodes of the sitcom, someone suggested that Ellen's character get a puppy — an idea that was rejected. The real-life Ellen also came out as a lesbian on the April 14, 1997, cover of *Time* with the words, "Yep, I'm Gay." Lots of rumors preceded the coming-out, something that Ms. DeGeneres had fun with, at one time saying, "Yes, the rumors are true. We'll be revealing that my character is Lebanese because she enjoys both baba ganoush and Casey Kasem." At the time, comedian Rosie

O'Donnell had not publicly come out of the closet, and she teased people by saying that she really liked Casey Kasem, and so "maybe I'm Lebanese, too."[106]

• Lesbian comedian Sabrina Matthews is very out. Sometimes, after watching her act, straight people will tell her, "I never met a gay person before." Ms. Matthews replies by stating the obvious, "Yeah, you did — you just didn't know it." She is also an activist who doesn't mind scaring straight people when they deserve to be scared. One day, in Provincetown, Massachusetts, she noticed a straight family with a father, mother, and young son and daughter. Nothing wrong with that, of course, but this particular father was pointing at and making fun of gay people. Therefore, Ms. Matthews snuck up behind him and whispered ominously in his ear, "How much for the girl?"[107]

• Lesbian comedian Vicki Shaw once appeared in a club where the manager — a gay man — told her not to do jokes about gays, although her jokes were gay friendly. Meanwhile, he had not told the straight male comedians appearing with her not to do gay material, although their jokes were anti-gay. Ms. Shaw told the manager, "If I can't do gay material, then they can't do gay material. It's those jokes that tell the redneck drunk that it's OK to go out and hunt some queers. ... if those rednecks are out in their truck looking for gays to beat up and you and I are walking down the street, guess who they're gonna pick?" The manager allowed her to do her gay-friendly material.[108]

• British gay comedian Alan Carr's on-stage persona is very much the same as his real-life off-stage persona. Once, as Mr. Carr was about to perform, someone told him, "So I'll just leave you 10 minutes so you can get into character." Mr. Carr replied, "Pardon?" Mr. Carr is an out comedian, but he does not specifically talk about being gay in his act. His gayness is simply there. When he is off-stage, occasionally drivers will yell at him, "Faggot!" Mr. Carr says, "I haven't been called that since I was at school, so actually I get all nostalgic."[109]

• Lesbian comedian Kate Clinton usually does not believe in outing homosexuals who don't want to be outed, but sometimes more important things — such as politics — make her want to out some of her fellow homosexuals. For example, after singer Ricky Martin was seen being chummy with George W. Bush at his first Presidential Inauguration, Ms. Clinton says that she started going into record stores, hanging around big advertisements for Ricky Martin's newest album, and telling passersby, "Did you know he's a big fag?" (Later, Mr. Martin outed himself.)[110]

• Gay comedian Bob Smith sometimes attends the Gay Pride festivities of Juneau, Alaska, where straight people celebrate alongside gays and lesbians. He once saw a hot man sitting at a bar during the Pride festivities and asked a friend who the hot guy was. This reply came back: "Oh, he's a fisherman. He's straight, but he doesn't care. A party's a party to him." By the way, at Juneau Mr. Smith saw a Yukon lesbian folksinging group, and as you might expect, they were called the Klondykes.[111]

• When homophobic people tell lesbian comedian Judy Carter that she just hasn't slept with the right person yet, she replies, "You're right. Do you know any cute homos who would be right for me?"[112]

Good Deeds

• When Billy Crystal was attending Marshall University in Huntington, West Virginia, he hosted a jazz show on the campus radio station, but he ran into a problem: a severe lack of jazz records. According to Mr. Crystal, in West Virginia Roy Clark is considered a jazz musician. (Keep in mind that Mr. Crystal is a professional comedian.) To solve his problem, he wrote a letter to John Hammond, the head of Columbia Records, a music company that has recorded many great jazz records. In the letter, Mr. Crystal mentioned his father and uncle, who had both been involved in a major way in jazz. (He says that he also mentioned Roy Clark and what West Virginians thought of him.) In response, Mr. Hammond sent Mr. Crystal 50 classic

Columbia jazz albums along with a catalog and an offer for Mr. Crystal to buy more jazz albums at the low price of $1 each.[113]

• Bill Cosby sometimes does favors for friends. One of the kids he grew up with is Bootsie Barnes, who became a professional saxophone player. He played mostly in small clubs for little money, but Mr. Cosby invited him to open for him at the Jones Beach Theater on Open Island, where Bootsie was able to play for 10,000 appreciative people. In Reno, Nevada, one of Bill Cosby's friends from before he became really famous opened up a McDonald's. To help make the opening a success, Mr. Cosby showed up, wearing a red jogging outfit, and signed autographs. One little girl saw his red jogging outfit and asked, "Is that Santa Claus?" Her mother replied, "No, dear, that's Bill Cosby. He's *better* than Santa Claus."[114]

• When comedian Margaret Cho was just starting out, she often was too timid to go into the green room (the place where entertainers hang out as they wait to perform — and after their performances); therefore, she would hang around outside the door. One day, the green room was empty, so Ms. Cho and some of the other newby entertainers she had met standing outside the door went in and had a seat. When she became a star, Ms. Cho invited into the green room any newby entertainers she saw timidly hanging around the door.[115]

• While entertaining the Desert Storm troops, comedian Jay Leno used to eat military food in mess halls and tease the troops by exclaiming, "Boy! This stuff is delicious! What is this — Thanksgiving dinner? I can't *believe* you guys are complaining!" The soldiers responded by throwing spoons at him. They also gave him a list of people — spouses, parents, other family members, boyfriends or girlfriends — to call when he returned to the United States. Mr. Leno personally made all the calls they requested.[116]

• As a child actor, Hector Gray had a chance to work with comedian Stan Laurel, of Laurel and Hardy fame, in England. He remembers that Mr. Laurel was very kind to the children, and he often took them — a few at a time — on trips to see sights. He was also very generous and bought them many children's books as gifts.[117]

Hair

• While working at Darmstadt, Rudolf Bing knew a comedian who was completely bald, but had three wigs with different lengths of hair. The comedian would wear the short-haired wig for a while, then the medium-haired wig. When he finally put on the long-haired wig, he would tell everyone he needed a haircut. Whenever the comedian began to wear the short-haired wig again, everyone complimented him on his haircut.[118]

• When he was a youngster, Billy Crystal loved the Beatles, and he wanted to grow his hair long like the Beatles wore their hair. Therefore, when he went to the barbershop, he always asked his barber to leave his hair long in back. Unfortunately, every time he went to the barbershop, the barber cut his hair short everywhere, including in back. When Billy complained, the barber would explain, "Your mother called."[119]

Illnesses and Injuries

• On April 19, 2005, George Lopez received a new kidney that was transplanted from his wife's body into his. After the operation, he joked, "Some people say that my wife and I are joined at the hip, but we're really joined at the kidneys!" His wife, Ann, denies that she is a hero because she gave one of her kidneys to her husband. Instead, she says that someone who gives a kidney to a person he or she does not even know is the real hero. Of course, Mr. Lopez, the star of the TV sitcom *The George Lopez Show*, is a very famous person. Even though he checked into the hospital under a pseudonym, Tom Ace, he was recognized. When someone called him by his pseudonym, the janitor said, "Hey, *loco*, that's George Lopez." Actually, Mr. Lopez himself was fooled by his own pseudonym. After the operation, the nurses were yelling, "Mr. Ace, wake up!" Mr. Lopez thought at first that they were yelling at someone else to wake up.[120]

• In January 1960, Zero Mostel nearly lost his left leg after an accident in which a city bus skidded into him. Doctors wanted to amputate, but Dr. Joseph Walker, Chief of Surgery for Joint Diseases at Knickerbocker Hospital, managed to save the leg. Later, Dr. Wilder gave a presentation to a group of surgeons and Mr. Mostel was present to show the results of the surgery. Wilder asked Mr. Mostel, "Please show the leg," and Mr. Mostel promptly pulled up his right pajama leg, showing a perfect leg. The surgeons had begun a standing ovation, when Dr. Wilder said to Mr. Mostel, "I'll kill you." Mr. Mostel then raised the left pajama leg, revealing a leg covered with scars. Dr. Wilder then received only light applause.[121]

• Nightclub comedian Joe E. Lewis got sick, was rushed to the hospital, and had to have an operation. His friend Frank Sinatra was there as Mr. Lewis was being wheeled into the operating room. Mr. Lewis asked him, "What's the prognosis? Don't b*llsh*t me." Mr. Sinatra replied, "You've got about a 50-50 chance." Mr. Lewis yelled, "Get me out of here! I want better odds than that!" Everyone laughed.[122]

• Steve Moore is an HIV-positive gay comic who laughs at the dark side of life. Once, a woman friend had a mastectomy. Of course, after her operation she was surrounded by very sorrowful and excessively solicitous friends, so it was a relief when Mr. Moore walked in to visit her and said, "Hey, Nancy — nice tit." She laughed.[123]

Language

• Comedian Lenny Bruce took comedy into controversial areas it had never ventured into before. He was concerned about language, and he once asked a nightclub audience, "Are there any niggers here tonight?" Of course, the crowd was shocked, but Mr. Bruce argued that such words as "nigger" were shocking and insulting because they had been suppressed. According to Mr. Bruce, "If President Kennedy said, 'I'm considering appointing two or three of the top niggers in the country to the cabinet,'" the n-word would soon lose both its shock value and its ability to insult. (In the audience was a shocked African-American comedian named Dick Gregory, who later titled his own autobiography *Nigger*. He also told Mr. Bruce's publicist, "This guy is the eighth wonder of the world. You have to go back to Mark Twain to find anything remotely like him. And if they don't kill him or throw him in jail, he's liable to shake up the country.")[124]

• Between 1935 and 1940, Buster Keaton was making films in foreign countries. Movies had sound then, so he recorded the movies in various languages, learning a sentence in one language and recording it, and then learning that sentence in another language and recording it, and so on. For one movie, he recorded the dialogue in French and in Spanish, and he did OK. But his German language instructor noticed a problem with his German: "Oh, I understand him very well, only he's speaking with a French-Spanish accent."[125]

• Near the end of his life, Monty Python member Graham Chapman used to go to college campuses where he showed film clips of his work and told anecdotes. (The author of the book you are reading now saw Mr. Chapman when he appeared at Ohio University in Athens, Ohio.) He usually began his talk by asking his audience to hurl verbal abuse at him for ten seconds. Why? According to Mr. Chapman, "It would certainly save a lot of time later on."[126]

• In his stand-up act, comedian Drew Carey uses a lot of profanity, but of course on his TV sitcom *The Drew Carey Show* he could not use nearly as much profanity as he does in his stand-up comedy. In fact, he remembers his first memo from the network censor, who wrote about the script for an episode, "Please note the excessive use of 'h*ll' and 'd*mn' found on pages 4, 20, 21, 22, 28, 38, 40, and 52, and reduce this number by half."[127]

• Will Rogers developed his writing skills in vaudeville. At first his was a dumb act — meaning he didn't speak in it. However, Will wanted to impress his audience with the difficulty of some of his tricks — such as throwing two ropes simultaneously and roping both a horse and its rider — and so he began talking to the audience. The audience found Will and his Oklahoma accent pleasing, and he began to make jokes.[128]

• It can hurt you not to know your audience. Stand-up comedian Judy Carter once opened for Jim Nabors in Kansas, where she said, "You know what really p*sses me off?" Big mistake. Kansas audiences in general and Jim Nabors fans in particular find the word "p*sses" offensive.[129]

• Comedian Phyllis Diller was a frequent visitor to the Playboy Mansion in Chicago, Illinois. The door to the Playboy Mansion bears a brass plate with this Latin inscription: *"Si Non Oscillas, Non Tintinnare."* ("If You Don't Swing, Don't Ring.")[130]

Laughs

• Who wrote the world's funniest joke? English comedian Spike Milligan did. No, that's not personal opinion. A professor studied this subject. Richard Wiseman, of the University of Hertfordshire, posted several jokes online, then asked people to vote on which one was the funniest joke. Over 300,000 people from all over the world did just that. Later, after the results were tallied, Professor Wiseman saw some 1951 footage of the Goons in their very first television appearance. The footage showed the Goons doing a version of the joke voted funniest in the world. And Spike Mulligan had written the jokes in that footage. So what is the funniest joke in the world? Updated for modern times, it is this: Two people go hunting, and a terrible accident occurs, severely injuring and perhaps killing one of the hunters. The uninjured hunter gets on his cell phone and calls 911, then sobs as he says, "There's been a terrible accident, and the friend I was hunting with is dead!" The 911 operator replies, "Please be calm, sir. The first thing we need to do is to make sure that your friend is dead." The 911 operator hears silence on the telephone for a moment, then he hears the sound of a shot, and the hunter says, "OK. Now what?"[131]

• Buddy Hackett was dining with a group of comedian friends when a woman approached the table and said that she wanted to tell a joke. Mr. Hackett told her, "Lady, go tell your joke at a table where amateurs are sitting. We're professionals here. We got all the jokes we can handle." By the way, if you ever want to make a comedian angry, here's an excellent way to do it. Buddy Hackett almost had a role in Martin Scorsese's excellent movie *Goodfellas*. Mr. Scorsese even came over to Buddy's house and explained Buddy's role in the movie — he would be in the background telling part of a joke. Buddy walked over to a window, then invited Mr. Scorsese to come over and look at the view. Buddy asked him, "Isn't that a beautiful lawn?" Mr. Scorsese agreed that it was a beautiful lawn. Buddy then told him, "Take a real good look because you will never be back in this house again. *Part* of a joke! Get the f**k outta here!"[132]

• The Marx Brothers and Charlie Chaplin were, as you would expect, practical jokers. When they were in vaudeville, the Marx Brothers gave Mr. Chaplin a free ticket to their show. He showed up, but all during their act he ignored them and read a newspaper. Mr. Chaplin then gave the Marx Brothers free tickets to see him, but the Marx Brothers gave the tickets to some Hasidic Jews. Mr. Chaplin thought that the Marx Brothers had dressed up as Hasidic Jews with long beards and black hats and black clothing, and he performed magnificently, but the Hasidic Jews weren't into comedy, and they left in the middle of his performance.[133]

• Fellow comedian Eddie Cantor once wrote Groucho Marx asking which were the two biggest laughs he ever received. Groucho replied: "Briefly (and quickly) the two biggest laughs that I can recall (other than my three marriages) were in a vaudeville act called 'Home Again.' One was when Zeppo came out from the wings and announced, 'Dad, the garbage man is here.' I replied, 'Tell him we don't want any.' The other was when Chico shook hands with me and said, 'I would like to say goodbye to your wife,' and I said, 'Who wouldn't?'"[134]

• In 1956, the Olympics came to Australia — so did satirist Stan Freberg. He opened his comedy concerts by parodying the carrying of the Olympic torch, which was then making its way from town to town in Australia. Mr. Freberg, wearing a blue suit, would arrive at the comedy concert venue carrying the Olympic torch and make his way to the stage — where he allowed a confederate to use the torch to light his cigar.[135]

• Ben Blue did a bit in his act as Chandu the Magician that George Burns considered hysterically funny. Mr. Blue put a man into a big basket, raised the basket about 15 feet above the stage, then he shot through the basket. "Blood" began dripping onto the stage, but Mr. Blue ignored the blood. As Mr. Burns wrote, "For the rest of the act, it kept dripping down. It was a riot."[136]

• At his first rehearsal at Glyndebourne, noted conductor Fritz Busch raised his baton, then he lowered his arm before even a note had been played, and joked to the orchestra, "Already is too loud."[137]

Letters and E-mails

• In 2007 and in some previous years, Gabe Kaplan, former star of *Welcome Back, Kotter*, considered himself a D-list celebrity. No problem. No one needs to be an A-list celebrity to lead a life of wit and intelligence. When Mr. Kaplan received an e-mail asking him to fight another D-list celebrity in *Celebrity Boxing*, he knew that he would reject the invitation, but he wanted to do so in a funny way. Therefore, he e-mailed back a list of silly demands that would have to be met before he would fight. For example, he claimed that he had become a Hasidic Jew; therefore, when he fought, he would have to wear a skullcap and a tzitzit, which Mr. Kaplan explains is "a body prayer shawl worn under a shirt so that only the fringes are visible." To his surprise, his silly demands were taken seriously. This gave him the idea to see what a D-list celebrity could get away with. He contacted a reputable book publisher, claiming that he had broken Wilt Chamberlain's record of sleeping with 20,000 women. The book publisher took his claim seriously. He contacted the Postmaster General's office, saying that he was a good candidate to be the first living person whose image would appear on a U.S. postage stamp. The Postmaster General's office thought he was serious. He contacted Sioux City, Iowa, to see if they would be willing to throw him a gala birthday parade, complete with floats. The good people of Sioux City, Iowa, were willing. Eventually, he got the idea of putting his e-mails and their responses into a book. Most people were good sports and gave him permission — and the good people of Sioux City, Iowa, let Mr. Kaplan know that they were still willing to throw him a gala birthday parade, complete with floats. Therefore, in 2007 Mr. Kaplan celebrated his birthday with a gala parade in Sioux City, Iowa. (By the way, Mr. Kaplan's book is titled *Kotter's Back: E-mails From a Faded Celebrity to a Bewildered World*.)[138]

• Hunter "Patch" Adams, M.D., once wrote a fund-raising letter for a charity. The 2-page letter, which was actually mailed and which was successful in raising funds, was entirely written in Greek. Why did he do this? He explains that he gets "so many fund-raising letters that they all start to look the same and they might as well be in Greek."[139]

Media

• When Kathryn Grant — the future Mrs. Bing Crosby — was 18 years old, she had a chance to interview famous stars Bob Hope and Joan Fonteyn. Unfortunately, she nearly caused a disaster by asking Ms. Fonteyn how old she was. Fortunately, Mr. Hope smoothed things over by saying, "Making allowances for your youth and inexperience, we still can't let you talk to a great star that way. Now, here's what you should have asked." Mr. Hope then asked Ms. Fonteyn a series of questions that both elicited the information needed for the future Ms. Crosby to write an interesting newspaper column and flattered Ms. Fonteyn at the same time. Ms. Crosby writes, "It was a gentle and instructive rebuke from a master craftsman, and I never forgot the lesson that it instilled. Months later, when the callow teenager interviewed Bing for her paper, she was ready to snare a superstar and a husband with a far more subtle approach."[140]

• As a boy, W.C. Fields had a unique way of peddling newspapers. He juggled the folded newspapers, and he yelled out teasers about the stories inside the newspapers. However, he ignored regular news stories and instead boosted unusual stories, such as "Bronislaw Gimp acquires license for two-year-old sheepdog. Details on page 26."[141]

• Lesbian comic Robin Tyler had an interesting early career. She became a Judy Garland impersonator at a bar for gay men in New York. After the police raided the bar, she was arrested along with several men in drag. The New York Post ran this odd headline: "44 Men and 1 Woman Arrested for Female Impersonation."[142]

Mishaps

• Being one of the Three Stooges — Moe, Larry, and Curly — sometimes involved sacrifice. In 1936, the Stooges made the comedy short *Ants in the Pantry*. In it, the Stooges are pest exterminators, but business is slow, so their boss finds a way to get more customers: "If they don't have any bugs, *give* them some!" Therefore, the Three Stooges start putting mice, ants, and moths in future customers' houses. During filming, a container of red ants broke in Moe's pocket, and they started swarming inside his clothing, leading to a lot of squirming by Moe. The director, Preston Black, loved it, saying, "Great, Moe! Keep up that squirming!" Moe remembers, "It was very funny — to everyone but me." Also in 1936, the Stooges made *Slippery Silks*. In this short, over 150 pies were thrown, and Moe ended up with a sore arm and a sore face because the pies that he did not throw were thrown at him. The other Stooges also suffered injuries: Larry lost a tooth while making one short, and Curly once got hit in the head while making a short and had to be attended to by a doctor. The doctor cut away some of Curly's hair so he could attend to his wound, and then he glued back the hair so Curly could resume shooting the short. (Curly is usually bald, but in a few shorts he has hair.)[143]

• Jane Russell and Bob Hope once entertained at the Paramount Theater in New York. Ms. Russell had trouble dropping off to sleep — too many drunks made noise in the hallways of her hotel across the street. One day she overslept, threw a fur coat across her nightgown, and then ran across the street where Mr. Hope was getting ready to introduce her. Standing in the wings, Ms. Russell threw open her fur coat, showing Mr. Hope her nightgown. Mr. Hope giggled, then told several more jokes, giving Ms. Russell time to put on a sequined gown and some lipstick.[144]

• Christa Miller co-starred as the character Kate in *The Drew Carey Show*. One day, she complained about an odor in her trailer. She had checked the refrigerator, but the odor was not coming from there. Another co-star of the show, Ryan Stiles, asked whether she had checked the microwave. She had not, and when she did check the microwave, she found roast beef that had been sitting there — and rotting — for over a week.[145]

• Homero Blancas once hit a bad shot that bounced off a palm tree and ended up in the bra of a spectator. He asked Chi Chi Rodriguez what he should do. Chi Chi replied, "I think you should play it."[146]

Chapter 4: From Money to Practical Jokes

Money

• Lesbian comic Rebecca Drysdale went to Sarah Lawrence College, and she fell in love with comedy and show business. Also attending Sarah Lawrence was Jordan Peele, now of *MADtv* fame. The two ignored classes, choosing instead to spend time improvising together. Eventually, Ms. Drysdale said to Ms. Peele, "I'm going to Chicago [to Second City]. Do you want to come?" Ms. Peele was willing: "Yeah. All right. Let me just go get my hat." Ms. Drysdale does well, but occasionally — the result of pursuing a career that lacks a steady paycheck — she needs to borrow money from her parents. Of course, she has promised to pay them back — and to buy them a house in the south of France. Now, whenever she needs to borrow money, the house in the south of France gets a little bigger. When her father hands over the money, he says, "Well, that's the fountain. That's the art studio, the music room." Ms. Drysdale says, "It's turning into an extremely nice house in the south of France. But I will make good on it."[147]

• Comedian Fred Allen was generous with handouts to moochers, and whenever he went out, he stuffed dollar bills into his pockets to give away. Of course, his reputation for generosity became well known, and moochers used to wait for him so they could cadge a dollar handout. Being human, Mr. Allen sometimes grew tired of always being hit up for cash, so when he left his NBC studio, he tried to outwit the moochers by leaving through a different door, choosing one of eight widely separated exits. But whatever way he exited the building, the moochers were waiting. Eventually, he figured out that the moochers had placed a spotter inside NBC. Mr. Allen would head toward an exit, and the spotter would rush outside and tell the moochers which exit Mr. Allen was using.[148]

• Comedian Jackie Gleason spent lots of money even when he didn't have lots of money. He had a tab at the Villa Capri in Hollywood, where he ran up the bill until he owed the Villa Capri owner, Patsy D'Amore, $5,000 — a huge amount of money in 1950. He then left Hollywood — and his unpaid bill — for three years. When he returned, he invited some friends at dinner at the Villa Capri, where they ran up a bill of $75. Mr. Gleason then wrote a check for $6,000 and gave it to Mr. D'Amore, saying, "I'm a big tipper." In addition, Mr. Gleason once ran up so big a tab at the bar of his friend Toots Shor that he told Toots that he felt like he couldn't use his signing privilege anymore. Toots, a true friend, told him that if he didn't want to sign his own name, then he should sign Toots' name. Mr. Gleason borrowed $20 from Toots, used it to tip some servers (a big tip), then joked, "Hey, I personally am always good for a C-note [$100], but you guys all know how cheap Toots is."[149]

• British music-hall comedian Ken Dodd made people laugh for over 50 years, debuting in 1954 and still entertaining at the end of 2007. Unfortunately, he did get in trouble with the tax people in the late 1980s because of £700,000 in 20 offshore bank accounts — which he allegedly had not declared. Of course, because he is a comedian, his trial (which ended with him being declared not guilty) had some light moments. For example, at one point the judge asked him what £330,000 in a suitcase felt like. Mr. Dodd replied, "The notes are not heavy, m'lud." Mr. Dodd is a gifted comedian. One of his best jokes is this: "Men's legs have a terribly lonely life — standing in the dark in your trousers all day."[150]

• In 1915, Eddie Jackson, a singer who later teamed with Jimmy Durante and Lou Clayton and performed comedy, worked in a bookbindery in Brooklyn under a foreman whose name was Al Capone. Mr. Capone liked to bet on horse races, but he wasn't good at it, so he often borrowed money from Mr. Jackson. Eventually, Mr. Jackson quit the job at the bookbindery, and eventually, Mr. Capone became a famous gangster in Chicago, but Mr. Capone didn't forget Mr. Jackson. Whenever Mr. Capone returned to New York for a visit, he would see Mr. Jackson perform and throw $100 bills at him.[151]

• Jack Benny often gave the biggest laughs to other members of the cast — he wanted laughter, and he wasn't particular who got it. (This is a characteristic of Mary Tyler Moore on *The Mary Tyler Moore Show*.) Other comedians wanted to be the ones who got the laughs. Once, a leading comedian read a script for his radio program, then angrily complained to his writers that the script made him the highest-paid straight man in show business. Writer Goodman Ace replied, "Jack Benny makes three times the money you do."[152]

• Comedians have various reasons for going on tour, including needing the money to buy a house. For example, Dawn French and Jennifer Saunders decided to go on one final tour as French and Saunders because Ms. French had seen a house in Cornwall that she wanted to buy, but she knew that she didn't have the money to buy it. Sometimes, the house is not for the comedian's personal use. Peter Kay went on a "Mum Wants a Bungalow" tour to raise money to buy his mother a house.[153]

• Jack Benny's comic persona was that of a man who is very tight with money — but in real life he was very generous. One night, he did a radio show in which his persona gave a large tip because he had forgotten his glasses. Following the show, Mr. Benny got into a taxicab, and when he paid his fare, he gave his usual large tip. The cabby, who had listened to the radio show, looked at the tip, then said, "You sure do need your glasses!"[154]

• Fred Allen lived frugally, although he gave away great sums of money to the poor and needy. When he decided to go to Hollywood, he wired an agent to find him and his wife a couple of rooms in an inexpensive hotel. The agent wired back, suggesting that he stay in a 12-room house. Mr. Allen responded with yet another telegram: "Don't be alarmed. You don't have to let on you know us."[155]

• Opera singer Frances Alda once made a fishing bet with Charlie Chaplin. First he bet her a dollar that she wouldn't catch any fish, then he said he would give her a dollar for every fish she did catch. After two hours of fishing, she had caught 83 fish, so he called off the bet and paid her $83. Ms. Alda knew she would win the bet — she hadn't told Mr. Chaplin that the flounder were running.[156]

• Comedian Jackie Gleason was a big spender, even if he had to borrow money to spend. He once borrowed $500 from friend and bartender Toots Shor, then ordered a limousine to drive him and Frank Sinatra fewer than 100 feet to a nightclub where one-armed trumpet player Wingy Malone was playing. Jackie kept giving Wingy $100 bills to play "That's a Plenty."[157]

• Comedian Lewis Black had a chance to perform at Villanova University, provided that he did not mock the Catholic Church. He replied that if Villanova would pay him $10,000, he would believe that the pope was infallible and anything else that Villanova wanted him to believe. Unfortunately, Villanova turned down his proposal.[158]

Mothers

• Comedian Adam Sandler had a good relationship with his mother as he was growing up. In the first grade, he would sometimes ask the teacher to excuse him, but instead of going to the restroom, he would go home. His mother never criticized him; she would simply make him a sandwich, and then walk him back to school. When Adam was eight years old, he entered and won a Punt, Pass, and Kick football tournament. However, because he wanted his mother to be proud of him, he waited for over 20 years to tell her how he won — he was the only competitor in his age group. Later, after he became a class clown and started getting poor grades, his mother yelled at him, "Why don't you ever try?" Adam recorded her, and then played the recording back to her. He says, "She laughed for half an hour."[159]

• Early in his life, Bernie Mac knew that he wanted to be a comedian. His mother was crying one day, the television was on, and comedian Bill Cosby made an appearance on *The Ed Sullivan Show*. Bernie was present, hoping that his mother would stop crying, and soon he saw that she was laughing at Bill Cosby even though her tears were still on her cheeks. A little later, she was laughing hard, and no one could tell that she had been crying. Although Bernie was only about four years old, he told his mother, "Mama, that's what I'm going to be. I'm going to be a comedian — so I don't ever have to see you cry."[160]

• Lesbian comedian Judy Gold is a mother who is very happy that children today are growing up with less prejudice toward homosexuals than their parents had. One day, a child had a play date with her young son. After going home, the child complained, "Why can't I have two moms?"[161]

• Comedian Bill Hicks discovered that he could get away with a lot on stage if he had the right comeback line. For example, he would do a joke about cunnilingus, shocking nearly everyone, then say, "My mother wrote that joke."[162]

• Comedian Bob Hope's mother was funny, too. One of the jokes his family told was that when Bob was born, his mother shouted to her husband, "William, get the doctor back. He's taken the baby and left the stork."[163]

Movies

• Buster Keaton came up with good gags, but he had to throw some of them out of his movies. For example, in *The Navigator*, he had a gag in which he had to repair his ship underwater, and a school of fish came near him. A big fish had trouble getting through the school of fish, so Buster acted like an underwater traffic cop. He took a starfish and let it attach itself to his clothing like a badge, and he then stopped the school of fish to let the big fish go on its way. (The gag took three days to film, and it took 1,500 rubber fish attached to violin string.) Unfortunately, the audience did not laugh at the gag because it occurred at a place in the movie where the audience thought that Buster ought to be serious — he had to fix the ship in order to rescue the heroine. Because the gag did not get a laugh when he previewed the movie, Buster deleted it from the movie. Don't feel bad for Buster, however — he put the gag in a trailer for the movie, and the gag got a big laugh.[164]

• Occasionally, a comic movie star will be so popular and work so hard that he or she seems to be ubiquitous — appearing in every comic movie. For comic movie star Ben Stiller, that happened in the mid-2000s. In 2006, Mr. Stiller starred in *Night at the Museum*, which was written by Thomas Lennon and Robert Ben Garant. When he was asked if Mr. Stiller was the actor they had in mind when he and Mr. Garant wrote the movie, Mr. Lennon replied, "We write every script with Ben Stiller in mind. If you work in Hollywood these days, you might as well."[165]

• Early in Lucille Ball's career, she had a small role in a movie titled *The Kid from Spain* that starred comedian Eddie Cantor. In the film, Mr. Cantor ducked and one of the glamour girls behind him got hit with a pie that had been meant to hit him. Lucy is the glamour girl who volunteered to get hit with the pie — none of the other glamour girls wanted to do the job. Later, Mr. Cantor told celebrity interviewer Joe Franklin that he knew on that day in 1932 that Lucy would go far in the business. Why? He explained that Lucy "wasn't afraid to be outrageous."[166]

• Opera singer Helen Traubel provided popular entertainment in addition to her better-known high-brow entertainment. She enjoyed both. For example, while making the film *Deep in My Heart*, she had the pleasure of working with the very funny Jim Backus, who was the voice of Mr. Magoo and a storyteller of renown. During a break, she laughed so hard that tears streamed down her face — a scene she filmed immediately afterwards had to be reshot because her mascara had also streamed down her face.[167]

• While filming the movie *Silver Streak*, Richard Pryor held on to Gene Wilder's belt while Mr. Wilder hung out of a moving train. During rehearsal, the train went 10 miles per hour, but during the actual filming, the train went 50 miles per hour. The stunt was dangerous, and Mr. Pryor made a promise to Mr. Wilder: If Mr. Wilder fell and was killed, Mr. Pryor would jump off the train.[168]

Music

• Comedian Steve Martin played banjo and performed magic during his stand-up days as a way to give his act a little extra. Later, he decided to get more serious about his music. In 2009, he spoke about solving a problem, "About 10 years ago I did something: I put a banjo in every room. So wherever I was, it was there. I didn't have to be in the mood to play the banjo and say, 'Oh, who wants to go back to the bedroom to pick it up?' It really helped me. You know, I started playing a lot more that way." Soon, opportunities came his way: banjo player Earl Scruggs requested that Mr. Martin play on one of Mr. Scruggs' albums, and *The New Yorker* asked him to host a banjo evening. In 2009, Mr. Martin went on tour with the North Carolina bluegrass band Steep Canyon Rangers, who are family friends. The tour is 85 percent music and 15 percent talking, but if some humor occurs to Mr. Martin, he throws it in.[169]

• Some people are brilliant, among them DustoMcNeato, aka Dustin McLean, who is a filmmaker in Pasadena. He says, "Ever wish songs just sang what was happening in the music video? Well now they do ...." DustoMcNeato had the idea of taking music videos and rerecording the lyrics so that what is sung simply states what is happening in the music video. Many people have borrowed this idea, and on <youtube.com> are a number of videos that give the "Literal Video Version" of famous songs. For example, DustoMcNeato's Literal Video Version of "Head Over Heels" by Tears for Fears contains these lyrics: "I've got a stack of books to return / I wish they were better / Now I'm singing in the library / And trying to flirt." Search <youtube.com> for "Literal Video Version" to see this and other videos of this kind.[170]

• Comedian John Cleese lacks musical talent and is completely unable to sing. Nevertheless, because of his comedic talents, he earned a role in the Broadway musical *Half a Sixpence* — with the understanding that he would mime as someone else did the necessary singing. However, after 50 performances, he felt comfortable with the role, so he began to join in the chorus — softly. After singing the chorus — softly — Mr. Cleese saw the musical's director, Stanley Lebowski, who scowled at him and asked, "John, are you *singing*?" Mr. Cleese admitted that he was, and Mr. Lebowski told him, "Well, don't."[171]

• The ivory keys of pianos can get very yellow when they get very old — at least, that's the usual explanation for the color. However, Victor Borge used to explain the yellow ivory keys on his piano by saying that the elephant had smoked too much.[172]

• Famed violinist Jascha Heifetz once tried to play Charlie Chaplin's violin, but it made a horrible noise. Mr. Chaplin then played it with his left hand doing the bowing, and it sounded beautiful. He had put all of the strings on backward.[173]

Names

• Comedian Albert Brooks and singer Linda Ronstadt used to date. Ms. Ronstadt has high praise for her former boyfriend: "He turned me into a real human being." Mr. Brooks agrees: "When I first met her, she was a Volvo." By the way, his father was radio comedian Harry Einstein, who named him Albert knowing that neighborhood kids would tease him by comparing him to the famed physicist Albert Einstein. Chances are, the teasing helped him become a comedian.[174]

• Groucho and Harpo Marx once managed a fighter who lost many more fights than he won. The Marxes promptly nicknamed him "Canvasback," but continued to manage his career. In one fight, Canvasback was knocked down five times in the first round. When the round was over, he tried to sit in the fighter's stool in his corner, but Harpo shoved him aside and sat down in his place, then Groucho fanned Harpo.[175]

• Mark Linn-Baker and Lewis Black used to perform comedy together at Yale University. More or less, they were performing so that they could get enough money to do their laundry. Therefore, they called their act *The Laundry Hour*.[176]

• Don Adams played Maxwell Smart in the 1960s TV series *Get Smart*. His real name was Donald James Yarmy, but actors were called in alphabetical order at auditions. He got tired of being called last, so he changed his name.[177]

Originals

• Whoopi Goldberg is a true original. While she was still in the process of being born, she put her thumb in her mouth, surprising the doctors and nurses. When she was a little girl, she asked her mother if she could be a princess. Her mother replied that an actress can be anything, and so Whoopi started acting. Her two cats were named Lou and Bud, after the comedians Lou Costello and Bud Abbot. And when she had her own talk show on TV, she invited white supremacist Thomas Metzger on. When he advocated the separation of the races, she asked him, "Where are you people going, 'cause I sure [...] ain't leaving."[178]

• Latino comedian George Lopez lives in a very fine house; after all, he is a multi-millionaire. In fact, he lives in such a fine house that many people, including many Latinos, are surprised that a Latino lives there — and owns it. He once needed a new roof, and so 15 Mexicans started working on it. In the afternoon, Mr. Lopez returned to his house and noticed that no one was working on the roof. He went looking for the Mexicans, and he found them having a party in and around his pool. One of the Mexicans saw him and said, "Hey, *vato* [dude], jump in. The man's not home."[179]

• Mel Brooks is the co-creator of the TV series *Get Smart*. One of his contributions to the series was the shoe phone worn by Control spy Maxwell Smart. The idea came to Mr. Brooks when every phone in his office started ringing, and as a joke he took off his shoe and started talking into it.[180]

Plagiarism

• The 1957 B-movie *Zero Hour* provided inspiration for the disaster movie spoof *Airplane!*, which was created by Jerry and David Zucker and Jim Abrahams, aka ZAZ. The movie featured a traumatized veteran being forced to land an airplane after the pilots and crew and passengers are made ill by food poisoning. In fact, many of the plot elements and even dialogue for *Airplane!* are taken directly from *Zero Hour*. For example, the line "We have to find somebody who cannot only fly this plane but who also didn't have fish for dinner" appears in both films. Paramount ended up buying the rights to *Zero Hour* so that it would not be accused of plagiarizing the film in *Airplane!*[181]

• Mel Brooks and Carl Reiner used to do a comedy routine in which Mr. Reiner interviewed Mr. Brooks, who played a 2,000-year-old man. However, they performed the routine only at private parties, not in public. Other comedians were impressed by the act. George Burns asked if the routine had been recorded on a comedy album yet. It hadn't, so Mr. Burns told them, "If you don't put it on an album, I'll steal it. I'm serious." They did, and it became famous.[182]

• Many comedians plagiarize, especially early in their careers. Early in his career, Jackie Mason introduced a comedian named Phil Foster. As he did so, he used much of Mr. Foster's own material. When Mr. Mason finished the introduction, Mr. Foster walked out on stage, said, "How do you do, ladies and gentlemen? You just heard my act, so good night." He then walked off the stage and left the building.[183]

• Ollie Joe Prator, a comedian from Michigan, stole other comedians' acts and did not even hide the fact that he was stealing their acts. He would go on the road, do another comedian's act, and tell the comedian later, "Man, you killed in Cleveland!"[184]

Politics

• Zero Mostel took the Fifth Amendment when questioned by the House Committee on Un-American Activities, perhaps in part because saying that he was not a Communist would have opened him up to prying questions about friends of his who may have been Communists. Certainly Mr. Mostel was a leftist when it came to politics. He survived the blacklist, partly by working as a nightclub comic at prices far lower than he had been receiving, partly by selling paintings, and partly because his wife went back to work. Late in life, he starred in *The Front*, a film about the blacklist that also starred Woody Allen. However, Mr. Mostel never forgave those who cooperated with the House Committee on Un-American Activities. Whenever he met an informer on the street, he called out cheerfully (but sarcastically), "Hello, Looselips!"[185]

• As a magician, Penn Jillette of Penn and Teller fame knows that it is possible to "force" a card upon a member of the audience when doing a card trick — that is, to make audience members choose the card the magician wants them to choose, although they think they are freely choosing that card. Occasionally, after Penn explains this, a member of the audience will protest that he really did freely choose a particular card. When this happens, Penn responds, "You must have loved the last election." (The book Mr. Jillette's quotation comes from was published in 1988.)[186]

• In 1948, Harry S. Truman won the election for President of the United States. He was already living in the White House, having become President after Franklin Delano Roosevelt's death. (Mr. Truman was Mr. Roosevelt's Vice President.) Many people had expected President Truman to lose the Presidential election and to have to move out of the White House. Following President Truman's upset victory, comedian Bob Hope sent him this short telegram: "UNPACK!"[187]

• Satirist Al Franken regularly made fun of disgraced President Richard Nixon, but when he produced a *Saturday Night Live*

"Presidential Bash" in 1992, he sent a letter to Mr. Nixon, hoping that he would make a personal appearance on the show. Unfortunately, as a reply, he received a letter saying no. No problem. Mr. Franklin happily framed the letter and now proudly displays it in a room that he has devoted to his collection of Nixon memorabilia: a bathroom.[188]

• Satirist Al Franken ran seriously for the United States Senate in 2007 in his native state of Minnesota. How seriously? Seriously enough to win. Even when he was in the 7th and the 8th grades, he was interested in politics, In the 8th grade, he gave weekly reports in his social-studies class about what was going on in politics, and in the 7th grade, he ran for Class President with the slogan, "Never spit in the face of a man unless his mustache is on fire."[189]

• Lewis Black and Ron, his brother, occasionally had arguments about politics. For example, Lewis was shocked when Ron told him that he was going to vote for H. Ross Perot for President. They started shouting at each other, and the argument ended with Lewis shouting, "Okay, you do that. You vote for H. F**king Ross Perot. And you know what I'm going to do? I'M GOING TO TELL MOM!"[190]

• Even back when he was a stand-up comic, Minnesota Senator Al Franken was interested in politics. Henry Kissinger once personally telephoned the offices of *Saturday Night Live* to request tickets to the show. Mr. Franken answered the phone and told him, "No." When Mr. Kissinger asked why he couldn't get the tickets, Mr. Franken told him, "Because of the bombing of Cambodia."[191]

• At an airport, lesbian comedian Kate Clinton was wearing a "John Kerry: A Stronger America" button during the 2004 Presidential election when a fundamental Christian couple came up to her and said, "A vote for John Kerry will hasten the Second Coming." Ms. Clinton replied, "Does that mean you will be leaving soon?"[192]

• While in high school, satirist Stan Freberg ran for student office and was elected on the strength of two campaign promises: 1) he would improve the principal's office by turning it into an automatic car wash, and 2) he would improve the girls' locker room by installing an 80-foot picture window.[193]

Practical Jokes

• Soon after he started working for *MAD* magazine, writer Dick DeBartolo needed an answer to a financial question, and only *MAD* publisher William M. Gaines, whom he had never met, could answer that question. His boss, Nick Meglin, called up Mr. Gaines — while Mr. DeBartolo was still on the telephone line — to arrange an appointment. Unfortunately, Mr. DeBartolo could hear every word Mr. Gaines said on the telephone: "DeBartolo's on the phone? Who the h*ll wants to speak to him? Did you tell him I'm in? Oh, Christ, what the h*ll does he want? He's a pain in the *ss!" Fortunately, when Mr. DeBartolo began speaking on the line, Mr. Gaines said, "Dick, I'm pulling your leg. Relax. I do that to all the new guys. I like to scare them. Welcome to *MAD*."[194]

• Ben Hecht once started a music group called the Ben Hecht Symphonietta. Its members consisted of several of his friends: Charles MacArthur, George Antheil, Charlie Lederer, and Harpo Marx. Groucho Marx was not invited to be a member, and it rankled him. As they were practicing in an upstairs room, Groucho yelled up at them, "Quiet, you lousy amateurs!" A few minutes later, no one could have heard the ensemble due to the vast sounds of music swelling up from the lower floor. Mr. Hecht and the other astonished musicians went downstairs to find the Los Angeles Philharmonic playing — Groucho had hired the entire orchestra to come and disrupt the rehearsal of the Ben Hecht Symphonietta.[195]

• Harpo Marx was a great friend of theatrical critic Alexander Woollcott, and when Harpo announced that he had taken up painting, Mr. Woollcott was enthusiastic and wanted to see some of his paintings. Harpo was willing, and one day Mr. Woollcott walked into Harpo's art studio. A nude female model was posing, and Harpo asked Mr. Woollcott to wait a few minutes as he put a few finishing touches on the paintings. So Harpo looked at the nude model and painted a little more, and then he allowed Mr. Woollcott to see the painting — which depicted not a nude model, but a banana.[196]

• Oscar Levant once became interested in the daughter of a Los Angeles society family, but she declined to date him until he and a member of his family were introduced to her family. Since no members of his family were in LA, Mr. Levant took along Harpo Marx when he visited her family and introduced Harpo as his uncle. Big mistake. Within five minutes, Harpo had insulted the butler, flirted with the maid, and chased the society woman's mother through the house. Of course, Oscar and Harpo were thrown out of the house as quickly as possible.[197]

• Comedians tend to play practical jokes on each other. While performing in the Ziegfeld Follies, Eddie Cantor was supposed to lift and carry around two empty suitcases, but during one performance they were enormously heavy — W.C. Fields had filled the suitcases with bricks. Mr. Cantor got Mr. Fields back by inviting him to play a game of golf, a game that Mr. Fields took seriously. But when Mr. Cantor took off his coat upon arriving at the gold course, he was wearing his pajamas and slippers and played the entire game in his jammies.[198]

• Occasionally, practical jokes are played during operatic performances. In a performance of *La Bohème* in Philadelphia, Frances Alda was surprised when her fellow singers turned toward her on stage with monocles in their eyes. When snow fell on stage, mixed with it were such items as buttons that hit the top of the bonnet she was wearing. A glass of water turned out to be a glass of ink. And when De Segurola put on a hat on stage, he discovered that it was filled with powder that cascaded over his shoulders.[199]

• Phil Silvers once played a joke on Jerry Lewis and Dean Martin. Mr. Silvers was suffering from insomnia in a hotel and suddenly remembered that the comedy team of Lewis and Martin was performing in the lounge. So he put on slippers and a robe, and walked into the lounge, where Lewis and Martin were in the midst of their wild shenanigans. The famous comedy team saw Mr. Silvers, stopped, and stared. Mr. Silvers said, "Fellas, could you hold it down a little? I'm upstairs trying to sleep."[200]

• Harpo Marx was always ready to make people laugh on the spur of the moment, and he often poked fun at dignified people. Once a dignified woman (whom Harpo didn't know) got out of a taxi in front of a hotel, and Harpo picked her up, ran with her to the hotel desk, and told the clerk, "Register us quickly!"[201]

• Practical joker Hugh Troy once heard the owner of a small general store say that he was due to take inventory soon. So Mr. Troy went to another store, bought $20 worth of items that the small general store carried, then smuggled them into the general store and put them on the shelves. Mr. Troy's name for his action was "Shop-stuffing. Makes a nice change from shop-lifting, don't you think?"[202]

• In Act 4 of Puccini's *La Bohème*, Mimi lies dying of tuberculosis, and Musetta gives her a muff to keep her hands warm. Frederick Jägel once surprised the singer playing the role of Mimi. When she slipped her hands inside the muff, she discovered a warm Polish sausage.[203]

• Comedian Brad Stein liked to sneak a couple of ketchup packets on board airplanes. After the plane had taken off, he would secretly squirt the ketchup below each ear, then point to his ears and ask the flight attendant, "Is this supposed to happen?"[204]

• When comedian Jay Leno, host of *The Tonight Show*, was in high school, he used to sneak into the girls' bathroom, pour water into the Kotex dispenser, then watch it expand and tear itself from the wall.[205]

Chapter 5: From Prejudice to Work

Prejudice

• British comedian Omid Djalili's family came from Iran, but he is not a Muslim (he is a Baha'i); however, because of his genetics, he looks foreign to some of his fellow Brits, and that can lead to misunderstandings. For example, at Heathrow Airport, he looked anxiously at two men who seemed suspicious to him: they were muttering and bearded. He then looked at his fellow Brits, and he saw that they were anxiously looking at *him*. He says, "I shouted at people and said, 'What are you looking at me for? Can't you see those blokes over there?' I had a real go at them, which made things worse. People just got upset and averted their eyes and I ended up muttering to myself." This story is important because, as British journalist Ginny Dougary writes, "One slight problem with this is that his bearded brethren were doubtless just as innocent as Djalili. But it's still a relief to hear a comedian having the guts to examine prejudice from his own perspective, only to demonstrate how he is also the victim of the same nervy thought poison."[206]

• Early in his career, Jewish comedian Milton Berle — then little more than an adolescent — worked on the same bill as Frank Fay, a comedian who was known for a lack of sensitivity. Because Frank Fay was annoyed that Milton was standing in the wings, he told the stage manager, "Get the little kike out of the entrance." Shocked, Milton complained to his mother, who told him that probably Frank Fay had said "tyke," not "kike." Milton then listened carefully to what Frank Fay said the next time the two were close together, and when Frank Fay told the stage manager, "I told you to keep that little Jew bastard out of the wings," Milton personally and immediately made sure that Frank Fay felt a strong urge to visit a hospital.[207]

• Many years ago, the Seacrest Hotel of North Falmouth, Massachusetts, was restricted — meaning that it did not welcome Jews.

When new managers took over the hotel, they decided to concoct a fictitious name for the new owner to show Jews that the hotel was no longer restricted. The name they decided on was Milton Q. Shapiro. Although "Milton Q. Shapiro" was completely fictitious and never existed, some would-be guests tried to bluff their way onto the premises when the hotel was filled to capacity by saying, "I'll have you know, I am a very close friend of Milton Q. Shapiro. He was a classmate of mine in college and a fraternity brother besides."[208]

• In *Chappell's Show*, comedian Dave Chappell attacked racism by playing such characters as a white supremacist who happened to be blind as well as black. Unfortunately, although most people recognized that racism was the real target of the subversive humor, some racists took it literally and congratulated Mr. Chappell for holding the same views that they did. Mr. Chappell was so shocked that he stopped making his TV show and stopped making the millions of dollars that went with making his TV show.[209]

• Kathy Nijimy and Maureen Gaffney are actor-comedians who created "The Kathy and Mo Show: Parallel Lives." They performed it at a lot of women's music festivals, where they discovered that gay people are just as likely as straight people to make assumptions about other people. At the women's music festivals, everyone assumed that Kathy and Mo were gay. In straight society, straights tend to assume that everyone is straight.[210]

• Brett Butler, star of TV's *Grace Under Fire*, once heard a bigot engaging in gay-bashing in a public place. She followed him outside and told him, "You've got to be really careful where you gay-bash." Of course, he asked, "Why?" She replied, "Because I know a lot of faggots who can kick your *ss — if the dykes don't get you first."[211]

• Stand-up comedian Laura Kightlinger has had nights when she has been on stage and men in the audience have called out to her such things as "Sit on my face" and "Show us your tits." Ms. Kightlinger says,

"In other words, I'm no different from any woman walking down the street."[212]

Problem-Solving

• Comedian Bill Hicks started performing before he could drive. He heard about amateur night at a club called the Comedy Workshop, so he called, asked for, and got permission to perform from the manager. Unfortunately, his parents told him that he couldn't perform. Not an insoluble problem. Bill sneaked out of the house through his second-story window and met a friend who was old enough to drive him to the club. Bill was popular with the comedians at the Comedy Workshop and with his classmates, but a principal heard his act, then told him, "You have the sense of humor of a 3rd-grader." Bill replied, "Well, then, you must have the comprehension of a 2nd-grader."[213]

• In 1965, the Friars Club, whose members are comedians, roasted Soupy Sales with comic insults. Mr. Sales and everybody else enjoyed themselves, but Friars Club member Brian Dougherty ran into a problem: He had to go to the bathroom, but he didn't want to miss any of the jokes. Fortunately, Mr. Dougherty is a problem-solver. He whispered to Marty Allen, who was sitting next to him at a table with an overhanging tablecloth, "Hand me that pitcher." With a relieved bladder, Mr. Dougherty was able to laugh even harder.[214]

• Early in his career, comedian Tim Conway worked with his friend Ernie Anderson in television in Cleveland, Ohio. Mr. Anderson had a locally produced, low-budget show called *Ernie's Place*; unfortunately, people did not want to appear on the show as guests. No problem. Mr. Conway simply appeared as the guest for each episode. His occupation changed from episode to episode, but his name remained the same — Dag Herford.[215]

• When country comedian Jerry Clower started to make it big in show business, he decided to get a fancy Rolex watch, but he discovered that all of them had Roman numerals on the watch face, and he didn't like Roman numerals. Fortunately, he was able to easily solve that problem. He hired a watchmaker to take a watch face from an inexpensive Sears and Roebuck watch and put it on the expensive Rolex watch.[216]

• Bob Woodruff, who once headed Coca-Cola, and ventriloquist Edgar Bergen went hunting. Both shot at a wild turkey, which fell dead, but both claimed to have made the shot that killed the turkey. Mr. Bergen said, "There's only one way to settle this." He picked up the dead turkey and asked, "Who shot you, turkey?" The turkey replied, "You did, Bergen."[217]

• When African-American comedian Chris Rock joined the cast of *Saturday Night Live*, he noticed that when he wore such clothing as jeans and a T-shirt or sweats, the security guards would often ask him to show his ID. To solve that problem, Mr. Rock started dressing up in suits whenever he was around the set of *Saturday Night Live*.[218]

• Carl Reiner, creator, writer, and producer of *The Dick Van Dyke Show*, sometimes wanted an extra 15 seconds to save a good joke when an episode was a little too long. He once saved a good joke by going through an episode and cutting a single frame from each scene.[219]

• The Domestic Resurrection Circus ends each year with an exorcism of one of the forces of evil. One year, a Mother Earth puppet set the military-industrial complex on fire. Another year, the Specter of Hunger succumbed to a fiery death. Art and activism can make us feel better.[220]

Sports

• Bill Cosby was an athlete before he became a stand-up comedian and movie and TV star. He once became the high-jump champion of the Middle Atlantic Conference by psyching out his opponents. He had not been jumping well, managing to clear only about six feet. However, at the meet a bump was on the approach to the high jump, and a few athletes had complained about it. Soon, Bill's voice was heard coming loudly from a tent: "There's really a terrible bump out there. There's no way anybody is going to jump over five-ten today." Mr.

Cosby won the championship with a jump of only six feet, which was actually a short height in that event.[221]

• Comedian Bernie Mac admires baseball player Pete Rose, aka Charlie Hustle. He tried to imitate Mr. Rose — once. Playing softball, he tried to steal second base. Trying to beat the throw to second, he slid headfirst — and tore off a bunch of skin on his chest. Normally, Mr. Mac's skin is black, but for a while after that slide, his chest was pink. Mr. Mac says about Charlie Hustle, "Now tell me he don't belong in the Hall of Fame."[222]

• Dick Van Dyke was tall at a very young age — 6-foot-1 at age 11. Because of his height, he tried out for the basketball team. However, he lacked coordination and warmed the bench all season. He had a chance to play in only one game — but unfortunately, when he jumped up to go on the court, his pants caught a splinter in the bench and the seat ripped out.[223]

Television

• The world's strangest comedian could very well be Andy Kaufman. One of his alter egos was Tony Clifton, an obnoxious jerk. While co-starring on *Taxi*, Mr. Kaufman wanted Tony Clifton to appear, but he insisted that he and Tony have separate contracts, separate dressing rooms, and separate parking spaces (although Mr. Kaufman, of course, was Tony Clifton). The good people at *Taxi* liked Mr. Kaufman, so they granted his wishes, but they soon discovered that Tony Clifton was not the right character to have on the show, so they decided not to use him. Mr. Kaufman, in the character of Tony Clifton, was outraged, and he yelled, "If you're going to fire me, you better bring security guards, and I want to be fired on stage." The good people at *Taxi* liked Mr. Kaufman, so they granted his wishes, and they fired Tony Clifton on stage. Mr. Kaufman, in the character of Tony Clifton, put on a great act, yelling at the *Taxi* head honchos, "You'll never work in this town again." Of course, security guards escorted Tony Clifton out of the building (just as Mr. Kaufman, in the character of Tony Clifton, had wanted), and soon afterward, Mr. Kaufman, in the character of Mr. Kaufman, walked in the building, acted like nothing had happened, and did not mention Tony Clifton.[224]

• Back when Johnny Carson was king of late-night television as host of *The Tonight Show*, Drew Carey — and every other standup comedian — dreamed of getting on the show. They also dreamed of being called over by Mr. Carson to sit on the couch — something he did only when he really, really liked a comedian's act. Unfortunately, Mr. Carey missed his first chance to be on *The Tonight Show*. While he was out of town, he did not check his messages, and when he returned to LA, he heard the message inviting him to be on *The Tonight Show*. He called *The Tonight Show* immediately, of course, but unfortunately they had already found another comic. The booker told Mr. Carey, "We'll get back to you." Mr. Carey took the mishap well, figuring that when *The Tonight Show* called again, he would have more experience and be funnier. Sure enough, *The Tonight Show* did call him again — two years later. Mr. Carey was very, very funny, and Mr. Carson invited him to sit on the couch. This TV appearance started many good things for Mr. Carey, who said, "I would take a bullet for Johnny Carson."[225]

• Ray Romano was happy when his TV sitcom *Everybody Loves Raymond* premiered. His wife, Anna, was in New York, and Ray was in Los Angeles. Ray decided to celebrate with a friend named Kevin James in Las Vegas, and he telephoned Anna to tell her, "Hey, my show aired last night. You know what? Millions and millions of people saw me on TV." Ray admits that at the time, "I'm just goofing around with this bravado." He then added in his conversation with Anna, "OK? So that's why I'm doing what I'm doing, 'cause I am a TV STAR." She told him, "You're still the d**k I married." Ray laughs and says, "That's good for me. There's somebody in my life you get the truth from." By the way, when the producer of *The Late Show with David Letterman* telephoned him to express interest in developing a TV sitcom around him — the sitcom that became *Everybody Loves Raymond* — the producer said,

"Just want you to know we're interested. Don't sign with anybody else because we're interested." Ray replied, "There IS nobody else."[226]

• *The Bob Newhart Show* is a much-beloved TV sitcom featuring Mr. Newhart as psychologist Bob Hartley and Suzanne Pleshette as Emily, his wife, a schoolteacher. In the sitcom, Bob and Emily are childless because Mr. Newhart did not want a show where the children use big words and are much more intelligent than their lovable but bumbling father. However, for the 6th season of the show, Mr. Newhart read a script in which Emily announced that she was pregnant. When he was asked what he thought about the script, he replied, "I think it's a very funny script — who are you going to get to play the part of Bob?"[227]

• Performers in television need to make their marks; that is, they need to stand in certain spots so that the camera operators can properly do their jobs. However, some performers in the days of live television declined to worry about making their marks. For example, comedian Jackie Gleason moved where the spirit moved him. When a camera operator complained, Mr. Gleason told him, "Well, pal, since I'm the star of this show, and your camera has wheels, just who in the h*ll do you think is going to move their *ss?"[228]

• Tommy Smothers, one of the two famous Smothers Brothers, was a genius at overcoming censorship. Back when satirist Pat Paulsen was running for President, network censors were very nervous about what Mr. Paulsen might do and say. As a producer, Tommy made Mr. Paulsen fidget during tapings, thus accomplishing two things: 1) making Paulsen the politician appear shifty, and 2) making editing the tapes impossible because of the technological limitations of the 1960s.[229]

• Groucho Marx could be cynical about such things as politicians and marriage, but when satirist Paul Krassner asked him what gave him hope, Groucho answered, "People." Of course, Groucho met many people as the host of *You Bet Your Life*, and his favorite contestant was an elderly gentleman who was happy. Groucho asked what made him happy, and the elderly gentleman replied, "Every morning I get up, and I make a choice to be happy that day."[230]

• Comedian Martin Short has created many characters, including his favorite, talk-show host Jackie Rogers, Jr., whom he created when he was just a kid. Often, he would perform a variety show with Mr. Rogers as host. The venue was his family's attic, and the audience was a tape recorder. Mr. Short says, "In my mind, I would see this show airing on NBC-TV at 8:30 on Thursday nights. But it was only every other week because I was far too hip for weekly TV."[231]

• Larry David, one of the creators of *Seinfeld*, did not want the show to be one of the sentimental varieties of sitcoms in which everyone hugs at the end after learning a lesson. This is evident in the way in which *Seinfeld* showed that each of the main characters could at times be shallow and manipulative. In fact, people involved with the show wore jackets that bore this motto: "No Hugging, No Learning."[232]

• During an appearance on the quiz show *You Bet Your Life*, a man was completely paralyzed by stage fright and could not speak a word. Groucho Marx said to the audience, "Either this man is dead, or my watch has stopped."[233]

Travel

• Americans can be incredibly ignorant about other countries. When he was a young man, comedian Lewis Black traveled throughout Europe, and unfortunately in France he was able to speak very little French. He asked about the location of a bathroom, but the French proprietor of the very inexpensive lodgings simply pointed to an odd contraption that looked like a toilet without a seat but with running water. Mr. Black crapped in the contraption, and he learned that it is a bad idea to crap in a bidet because you have to clean the crap up. Of course, people from other countries can also be ignorant about the United States. Mr. Black's grandfather emigrated to the U.S., where he once got in trouble because he had not paid his taxes. When the tax people informed him, "You have to pay taxes every year," he replied, "Really? I didn't know."[234]

• Life on the road can be hard for a stand-up comedian. For a while, Margaret Cho was so busy that she often woke up not knowing in which city she was performing. Whenever that happened, she would look for a telephone book to find out where she was. While sleeping in her own home, she occasionally had a nightmare about missing a flight. She would wake up, quickly get dressed and pack a bag, then realize that this was a rare day off and she didn't have to travel anywhere.[235]

• Comedian Rita Rudner once rented a house in the Kensington area of London, England. On her first morning in the house, she went to her terrace and looked out over the neighborhood, where she saw a group of horses sunning themselves. This sounds normal — but the horses were on the top-story balcony of a high-rise. No, this was not a drug-induced hallucination. The horses belonged to the Queen, and she kept them in this horses-only apartment building.[236]

• In 1939, the Three Stooges were invited to perform in London at the Palladium. They did not pay for first-class passage on the ship that took them to England, but the captain of the ship was a fan, so he upgraded them to first class at no cost to them. Moe Howard, the leader of the Stooges, remembers with amusement a newspaper headline that he saw when they arrived: "STOOGES ARRIVE IN LONDON — QUEEN LEAVES FOR AMERICA."[237]

• Humorist Frank Sullivan used to dream about sailing overseas, but unfortunately, he never did because he suffered from seasickness. He told a friend, "I doubt that I'll ever be cured, but I'll still hoping eventually to go abroad. Every day I'm stepping over larger puddles."[238]

• Jack E. Leonard, a much-overweight comedian, once squeezed into a taxicab and ordered the driver, "Take me to a larger cab."[239]

Wit

• Wikipedia is completely written by its users — volunteers all. Of course, as you may expect, some users try to post incorrect information. Often, this is funny misinformation. For example, in late October 2006, this information appeared in the entry for Essex High School: "At EHS students are free to do whatever they wish in their time after school. This policy has led to the creation of the Zombie Killing Squad, the Pro-Zombie Acceptance Committee, the Zombie Hate Club and the Debate Team." Fortunately (or perhaps unfortunately), this misinformation was quickly noticed and quickly deleted.[240]

• Back in the Vietnam War era, comedian Jackie Mason made fun of reports that we were winning the war. For example, to make fun of reports that we were bombing 500 bridges a week in Vietnam, he would say that he had recently returned from Vietnam, and there weren't but eight bridges in the whole country. Does that mean that we should disbelieve military reports? Not necessarily. Mr. Mason said that apparently the military first airdropped the bridges in Vietnam and then destroyed them.[241]

• David Letterman is known for his wit. As a member of the Sigma Chi fraternity, he once talked a fellow fraternity member into shaving his head and painting it blue. Mr. Letterman then pointed out the fraternity member to other people and said that he was the world's biggest ballpoint pen. And as a weather broadcaster in Indiana (early in his career), he once announced the temperatures of two cities — "Muncie, 42; Anderson, 44" — then said, "Always a close game."[242]

• Groucho Marx, master of insults, once toasted a socialite in this way: "I drink to your charm, your beauty, and your brains — which will give you a rough idea of how hard up I am for a drink." His brother Chico Marx was a master of chasing skirts. When his wife caught him kissing another woman, he explained, "I wasn't kissing her. I was whispering in her mouth."[243]

Work

• Chris Rock became a comedian almost as a fluke. In 1983, he wanted to see in person Eddie Murphy — a comedian whom he "totally idolized." While standing in line at Radio City Music Hall to buy a ticket, he read a local paper that included information about comedy clubs. Mr. Rock says, "I don't know what it was, but something in my head said [to] walk away, so I did." He walked to the comedy club Catch a Rising Star. Fortunately, it was audition night, and fortunately he drew a lottery number that allowed him to be one of the people who auditioned that night. While waiting to go on stage, he wrote some jokes, and he succeeded so well that he was offered work at the club. This was fortunate. Mr. Rock says, "I knew nothing. If he hadn't told me to come back, I never would have." Of course, Mr. Rock rose in the comedy ranks, and a big break came when Eddie Murphy saw his act and hired him to play the role of a valet in *Beverly Hills Cop II*. What would Mr. Rock be doing now if he had not listened to the voice in his head telling him to walk away? He says, "I don't know, driving a truck, something like that. But happy. I'd be a happy guy doing that."[244]

• In 1929, Laurel and Hardy made the short comedy film "Liberty," for which a three-story building was constructed. At one point, the comedy team was working 200 feet above ground, but a wooden platform below them was supposed to provide them safety. Mr. Laurel expressed concern about the height the comedy team was working at, so to prove that they were safe, Mr. Hardy jumped down on the wooden platform. However, the wood was made of flimsy sugar pine, and he fell through the platform. Fortunately, a competent crewmember named Thomas Benton Roberts, who had unsuccessfully complained about the flimsiness of the safety platform, had gone to the trouble of putting up a safety net below the safety platform — something he was not required to do. Instead of falling 200 feet, Mr. Hardy fell only 20 feet. He was shaken by the fall, but he quickly went back to work.[245]

• Bob and Ray, aka Bob Elliott and Ray Goulding, worked together for decades as comedians, and apparently the entire time they were trying to make each other laugh, and as a side effect they made their audiences laugh. According to Andy Rooney, who wrote a foreword to one of the collections of Bob and Ray's scripts, the two men "have three distinct personalities. There's Bob's, there's Ray's, and then there's Bob & Ray's." According to Mr. Rooney, when you met the two men separately, "two duller people you never talked to." And Chris Elliott, Bob's son, who is also a comedian, says that for years he thought his father was some kind of a businessman. Only at age 11 did Chris realize that his father worked as a comedian for a living. Of course, Bob and Ray were very close. Late in their career together, Ray joked, "I've been married to my wife for thirty-seven years, and to Bob for thirty-five."[246]

• Moe Howard of Three Stooges fame knew at an early age that he wanted to be in show business. When he was 17 years old, he ran across an advertisement in *Billboard* for an actor on a showboat. As part of the application process, he had to mail a photograph of himself. To improve his chances of getting a job, Moe did not use his own photo, but instead he sent the photo of a taller, more handsome friend. The plan worked — he got the job! Of course, the company manager who had advertised for the actor was surprised when Moe showed up — he did not at all look like the man in the photo he had mailed. But the company manager let Moe run errands for the actors, and when he did let Moe act in a few small roles, Moe was excellent.[247]

• Stand-up comedians need to have a lot of confidence that they can "get" an audience — that is, make an audience laugh. When Judy Carter worked as the opening act for Loggins and Messina, sometimes the music-loving audience did NOT want to hear her. Once, the opening of the show was delayed for an hour, so the audience was even more impatient than usual to hear the band. Things got so bad that a druggie member of the audience came up on stage, threw a tablecloth over Ms. Carter's head — then SET IT ON FIRE. As Ms. Carter was being carried off the stage to safety, she kept saying, "Put me down. I know I can get them."[248]

• Comedian Jimmy Durante started out in show business as a piano player. Singer and comedian Eddie Cantor was the first person to urge Jimmy to get up on stage and away from the piano: "Piano playing is going to get you nothing. You'll be a piano player till you're a hundred years old. You gotta look further than that. People like you a whole lot. So why don't you get up on the floor and say something to the people?" Eventually, of course, Mr. Durante took Mr. Cantor's advice. However, his immediate reaction was, "Gee, Eddie, I wouldn't do that. I'd be afraid that people would laugh at me."[249]

• Lesbian comedian Judy Gold once worked on the New Jersey turnpike as a toll collector. The job had its interesting moments. She points out, "It was the '80s, and people going to concerts at the Garden State Arts Center would give me joints." However, she also remembers a time when she had 12 trucks backed up in her lane. Why? She explains, "The guys would get on the CB and be like, 'Chick in lane four.'"[250]

Appendix A: Bibliography

Adams, Joey. *The Borscht Belt*. With Henry Tobias. New York: Avon Books, 1966.

Adler, Bill. *Jewish Wit and Wisdom*. New York: Dell Publishing Co., Inc., 1969.

Adler, Bill, and Bruce Cassiday. *The World of Jay Leno: His Humor and His Life*. New York: Carol Publishing Group, 1992.

Adler, Irene. *I Remember Jimmy: The Life and Times of Jimmy Durante*. New York: Arlington House, Publishers, 1980.

Alda, Frances. *Men, Women, and Tenors*. Boston, MA: Houghton Mifflin Company, 1937.

Allen, Steve. *But Seriously ....* Amherst, NY: Prometheus Books, 1996.

Allen, Steve. *The Funny Men*. New York: Simon and Schuster, Inc., 1956.

Alworth, E. Paul. *Will Rogers*. New York: Twayne Publishers, Inc., 1974.

Auerbach, Arnold M. *Funny Men Don't Laugh*. Garden City, NY: Doubleday and Co., Inc., 1965.

Bacon, James. *How Sweet It Is: The Jackie Gleason Story*. New York: St. Martin's Press, 1985.

Beach, Scott. *Musicdotes*. Berkeley, CA: Ten Speed Press, 1977.

Barreca, Regina, editor. *New Perspectives on Women and Comedy*. Philadelphia, PA: Gordon and Breach, 1992.

Bing, Sir Rudolf. *5000 Nights at the Opera*. Garden City, NY: Doubleday and Company, Inc., 1972.

Black, Lewis. *Me of Little Faith*. New York: Riverhead Books, 2008.

Black, Lewis. *Nothing Sacred*. New York: Simon Spotlight Entertainment, 2005.

Blue, Rose, and Corinne Naden. *Chris Rock*. Philadelphia, PA: Chelsea House Publishers, 2000.

Brown, Jared. *Zero Mostel: A Biography*. New York: Atheneum, 1989.

Bryan III, J. *Merry Gentlemen (and One Lady)*. New York: Atheneum, 1985.

Burns, George. *All My Best Friends*. Written with David Fisher. New York: Putnam Publishing Group, 1989.

Burns, George. *Wisdom of the 90s*. Written with Hal Goldman. New York: G.P. Putnam's Sons, 1991.

Cantor, Eddie. *The Way I See It*. Englewood Cliffs, NJ: Prentice Hall, 1959.

Cantor, Eddie, and David Freedman. *Ziegfeld: The Great Glorifier*. New York: Alfred H. King, Inc., 1934.

Carter, Judy. *The Homo Handbook*. New York: Fireside Books, 1996.

Carter, Judy. *Stand-Up Comedy: The Book*. New York: Dell Publishing, 1989.

Claus, S. *Holiday Cheer for the 19th Hole*. With help from Russ Edwards and Jack Kreismer. Saddle River, NJ: Red-Letter Press, 2003.

Claxton, William, photographer. *Laugh: Portraits of the Greatest Comedians and the Funny Stories They Tell Each Other*. Introduction by John Lithgow; conceived and produced by Andy Gould and Kathleen Bywater; text edited by Mike Thomas. New York: William Morrow, 1999.

Clinton, Kate. *What the L?* New York: Carroll & Graf Publishers, 2005.

Clower, Jerry. *Ain't God Good!* Waco, TX: Word Books, Publisher, 1975.

Clower, Jerry. *Stories from Home*. Jackson, MS: University Press of Mississippi, 1992.

Cox, Wally. *My Life as a Small Boy*. New York: Avon, 1961.

Crystal, Billy. *700 Sundays*. New York: Warner Books, 2005.

Dean, Greg. *Step by Step to Stand-Up Comedy*. Portsmouth, NH: Heinemann, 2000.

DeBartolo, Dick. *Good Days and MAD*. New York: Thunder's Mouth Press, 1994.

Diller, Phyllis. *Like a Lampshade in a Whorehouse: My Life in Comedy*. With Richard Buskin. London: Penguin Group, 2005.

Donaldson, William. *Great Disasters of the Stage*. London: Arrow Books, Limited, 1984.

Dougherty, Barry. *A Hundred Years, A Million Laughs*. Cincinnati, OH: Emmis Books, 2004.

Epstein, Lawrence J. *The Haunted Smile: The Story of Jewish Comedians in America*. New York: PublicAffairs, 2001.

Epstein, Lawrence J. *Mixed Nuts: America's Love Affair with Comedy Teams From Burns and Allen to Belushi and Aykroyd*. New York: PublicAffairs, 2004.

Feinberg, Morris "Moe." *Larry: The Stooge in the Middle*. With G.P. Skratz. San Francisco, CA: Last Gasp of San Francisco, 1984.

Feran, Tom, and R.D. Heldenfels. *Ghoulardi: Inside Cleveland TV's Wildest Ride*. Cleveland, OH: Gray & Company, Publishers, 1997.

Flowers, Charles, editor. *Out, Loud, and Laughing: A Collection of Gay and Lesbian Humor*. New York: Anchor Books, 1995.

Forwood, Margaret. *The Real Benny Hill*. London: Robson Books, 1992.

Franklin, Joe. *Up Late with Joe Franklin*. New York: Scribner, 1995.

Freberg, Stan. *It Only Hurts When I Laugh*. New York: Times Books, 1988.

Gaines, Ann Graham. *Drew Carey*. Philadelphia, PA: Chelsea House Publishers, 1999.

Garagiola, Joe. *It's Anybody's Ballgame*. New York: Jove Books, 1988.

Garner, Joe. *Made You Laugh: the Funniest Moments in Radio, Television, Stand-up, and Movie Comedy*. Kansas City, MO: Andrews McMeel Publishing, 2004.

Gray, Hector. *An Actor Looks Back*. Hobart Tasmania: Cat and Fiddle Press, 1973.

Green, Joey. *The Get Smart Handbook*. New York: Collier Books, 1993.

Green, Joey. *Hi Bob! The Unofficial Guide to* The Bob Newhart Show. New York: St. Martin's Griffin, 1996. Advance uncorrected proofs.

Greenberg, Keith Elliot. *Charles, Burrows, and Charles: TV's Top Producers*. Woodbridge, CT: Blackbirch Press, Inc., 1995.

Grudens, Richard. *The Spirit of Bob Hope: One Hundred Years, One Million Laughs*. Stony Brook, NY: Celebrity Profiles Publishing Company, 2002.

Guzmán, Lila and Rick. *George Lopez: Latino King*. Berkeley Heights, NJ: Enslow Publishers, Inc., 2009.

Guzzetti, Paula. *Jim Carrey*. Parsippany, NJ: Dillon Press, 1998.

Harmon, Jim. *The Great Radio Comedians*. Garden City, NY: Doubleday and Company, Inc., 1970.

Haskins, Jim. *Richard Pryor: A Man and His Madness*. New York: Beaufort Books, Inc., 1984.

Hayes, Kevin J., editor. *Charlie Chaplin: Interviews*. Jackson, MS: University Press of Mississippi, 2005.

Hecht, Andrew. *Hollywood Merry-Go-Round*. New York: Grosset and Dunlap, Publishers, 1947.

Hicks, Bill. *Love All the People: Letters, Lyrics, Routines*. Brooklyn, NY: Soft Skull Press, 2004.

Howard, Moe. *Moe Howard and the Three Stooges*. Secaucus, NJ: Citadel Press, 1977.

Iannucci, Lisa. *Ellen DeGeneres: A Biography*. Westport, CT: Greenwood Press, 2009.

Irving, Gordon, compiler. *The Wit of the Scots*. London: Leslie Frewin Publishers, Inc., 1969.

Jenkins, Ron. *Acrobats of the Soul*. New York: Theatre Communications Group, Inc., 1988.

Karvoski Jr., Ed. *A Funny Time to be Gay*. New York: Simon and Schuster, 1997.

Katz, Sandor. *Whoopi Goldberg*. Philadelphia, PA: Chelsea Juniors, 1997.

Kettelkamp, Larry. *Bill Cosby: Family Funny Man*. New York: Julian Messner, 1987.

Knotts, Don. *Barney Fife and Other Characters I Have Known*. With Robert Metz. New York: Berkley Boulevard Books, 1999.

Lefkowitz, Frances. *David Letterman*. New York: Chelsea House Publishers, 1997.

Levant, Oscar. *A Smattering of Ignorance*. New York: Doubleday, Doran, and Co., 1940.

Levenson, Sam. *Everything But Money*. New York: Simon and Schuster, 1966.

Linkletter, Art. *I Didn't Do It Alone: The Autobiography of Art Linkletter*. Ottawa, IL: Caroline House Publishers, Inc., 1980.

Lyman, Darryl. *The Jewish Comedy Catalog*. Middle Village, NY: Jonathan David Publishers, Inc., 1989.

Mac, Bernie. *I Ain't Scared of You*. With Darrell Dawsey. New York: Pocket Books, 2001.

Malloy, Merrit, and Marsha Rose. *Comedians' Quote Book*. New York: Sterling Publishing Co., Inc., 1993.

Manchel, Frank. *The Box Office Clowns*. New York: Franklin Watts, 1979.

Manchel, Frank. *Yesterday's Clowns: The Rise of Film Comedy*. New York: Franklin Watts, Inc., 1973.

Marcovitz, Hal. *Robin Williams*. Philadelphia, PA: Chelsea House Publishers, 2000.

Marx, Groucho. *Confessions of a Mangy Lover*. New York: Da Capo Press, 1997.

Marx, Groucho. *The Groucho Letters: Letters From and To Groucho Marx*. New York: Simon and Schuster, 1967.

Marx, Maxine. *Growing Up with Chico*. New York: Limelight Editions, 1986.

McGarry, Annie. *Laurel & Hardy*. Greenwich, CT: Chartwell Books, Inc., 1992.

Mingo, Jack. *The Juicy Parts*. New York: The Berkley Publishing Group, 1996.

Moore, Dudley. *Musical Bumps*. London: Robson Books, 1986.

Moore, Grace. *You're Only Human Once*. Garden City, NY: Doubleday, Doran and Co., Inc., 1944.

Morgan, David. *Monty Python Speaks*. New York: Avon Books, Inc., 1999.

Morton, Robert, editor. *Stand-up Comedians on Television*. New York: Harry N. Abrams, Inc. [in association with] The Museum of Television & Radio, 1996.

Mott, Robert L. *Radio Live! Television Live!: Those Golden Days When Horses Were Coconuts*. Jefferson, NC: McFarland & Company, Inc., Publishers, 2000.

Mullen, Tom. *Seriously, Life is a Laughing Matter*. Waco, TX: Word Books, 1978.

Nachman, Gerald. *Seriously Funny: The Rebel Comedians of the 1950s and 1960s*. New York: Pantheon Books, 2003.

Neuwirth, Allan. *They'll Never Put That on the Air: An Oral History of Taboo-Breaking TV Comedy*. New York: Allworth Press, 2006.

Nixon, Joan Lowery. *The Making of a Writer*. New York: Delacorte Press, 2002.

Pegg, Robert. *Comical Co-Stars of Television*. Jefferson, NC: McFarland & Company, Inc., Publishers, 2002.

Sales, Soupy. *Soupy Sez! My Zany Life and Times*. With Charles Salzberg. New York: M. Evans and Company, Inc., 2001.

Sales, Soupy. *Stop Me If You've Heard It!* New York: M. Evans and Company, Inc., 2003.

Samra, Cal and Rose, editors. *Holy Humor*. Colorado Springs, CO: WaterBrook Press, 1997.

Sanford, Herb. *Ladies and Gentlemen, The Garry Moore Show: Behind the Scenes When TV was New*. New York: Stein and Day, Publishers, 1976.

Schuman, Michael A. *Bill Cosby: Actor and Comedian*. Berkeley Heights, NJ: Enslow Publishers, Inc., 1995.

Scordato, Mark and Ellen. *The Three Stooges*. New York: Chelsea House Publishers, 1995.

Seidman, David. *Adam Sandler*. Philadelphia, PA: Chelsea House Publishers, 2001.

Smith, H. Allen. *Lost in the Horse Latitudes*. Garden City, NY: Doubleday, Doran, and Co., 1944.

Stuart, Andrea. *Showgirls*. London: Jonathan Cape, 1996.

Sullivan, Frank. *Well, There's No Harm in Laughing*. Garden City, NY: Doubleday & Company, Inc., 1970.

Sweeney, Kevin W., editor. *Buster Keaton: Interviews*. Jackson, MS: University of Mississippi Press, 2000.

Tiger, Caroline. *Margaret Cho*. New York: Chelsea House Publishers, 2007.

Topol, Chaim, compiler. *Topol's Treasury of Jewish Humor, Wit and Wisdom*. New York: Barricade Books, Inc., 1994.

Tracy, Kathleen. *Home Brewed: The Drew Carey Story*. New York: Boulevard Books, 1997.

Traubel, Helen. *St. Louis Woman*. New York: Duell, Sloan and Pearce, 1959.

True, Cynthia. *American Scream: The Bill Hicks Story*. New York: HarperEntertainment, 2002.

Underwood, Peter. *Danny La Rue: Life's a Drag!* London: W.H. Allen & Co., Ltd., 1974.

Van Dyke, Dick. *Those Funny Kids!* Garden City, NY: Doubleday and Company, Inc., 1975.

Vera, Veronica. *Miss Vera's Cross-Dress for Success*. New York: Villard Books, 2002.

Zehme, Bill. *The Way You Wear Your Hat: Frank Sinatra and the Lost Art of Livin'*. New York: HarperCollinsPublishers, 1997.

Appendix B: About the Author

It was a dark and stormy night. Suddenly a cry rang out, and on a hot summer night in 1954, Josephine, wife of Carl Bruce, gave birth to a boy — me. Unfortunately, this young married couple allowed Reuben Saturday, Josephine's brother, to name their first-born. Reuben, aka "The Joker," decided that Bruce was a nice name, so he decided to name me Bruce Bruce. I have gone by my middle name — David — ever since.

Being named Bruce David Bruce hasn't been all bad. Bank tellers remember me very quickly, so I don't often have to show an ID. It can be fun in charades, also. When I was a counselor as a teenager at Camp Echoing Hills in Warsaw, Ohio, a fellow counselor gave the signs for "sounds like" and "two words," then she pointed to a bruise on her leg twice. Bruise Bruise? Oh yeah, Bruce Bruce is the answer!

Uncle Reuben, by the way, gave me a haircut when I was in kindergarten. He cut my hair short and shaved a small bald spot on the back of my head. My mother wouldn't let me go to school until the bald spot grew out again.

Of all my brothers and sisters (six in all), I am the only transplant to Athens, Ohio. I was born in Newark, Ohio, and have lived all around Southeastern Ohio. However, I moved to Athens to go to Ohio University and have never left.

At Ohio U, I never could make up my mind whether to major in English or Philosophy, so I got a bachelor's degree with a double major in both areas, then I added a Master of Arts degree in English and a Master of Arts degree in Philosophy. Yes, I have my MAMA degree.

Currently, and for a long time to come (I eat fruits and veggies), I am spending my retirement writing books such as *Nadia Comaneci: Perfect 10*, *The Funniest People in Comedy*, *Homer's* Iliad: *A Retelling in Prose*, and *William Shakespeare's* Hamlet: *A Retelling in Prose*.

By the way, my sister Brenda Kennedy writes romances such as *A New Beginning* and *Shattered Dreams*.

Appendix C: Some Books by David Bruce

Anecdote Collections

250 Anecdotes About Opera
250 Anecdotes About Religion
250 Anecdotes About Religion: Volume 2
250 Music Anecdotes
Be a Work of Art: 250 Anecdotes and Stories
The Coolest People in Art: 250 Anecdotes
The Coolest People in the Arts: 250 Anecdotes
The Coolest People in Books: 250 Anecdotes
The Coolest People in Comedy: 250 Anecdotes
Create, Then Take a Break: 250 Anecdotes
Don't Fear the Reaper: 250 Anecdotes
The Funniest People in Art: 250 Anecdotes
The Funniest People in Books: 250 Anecdotes
The Funniest People in Books, Volume 2: 250 Anecdotes
The Funniest People in Books, Volume 3: 250 Anecdotes
The Funniest People in Comedy: 250 Anecdotes
The Funniest People in Dance: 250 Anecdotes
The Funniest People in Families: 250 Anecdotes
The Funniest People in Families, Volume 2: 250 Anecdotes
The Funniest People in Families, Volume 3: 250 Anecdotes
The Funniest People in Families, Volume 4: 250 Anecdotes
The Funniest People in Families, Volume 5: 250 Anecdotes
The Funniest People in Families, Volume 6: 250 Anecdotes
The Funniest People in Movies: 250 Anecdotes
The Funniest People in Music: 250 Anecdotes
The Funniest People in Music, Volume 2: 250 Anecdotes
The Funniest People in Music, Volume 3: 250 Anecdotes
The Funniest People in Neighborhoods: 250 Anecdotes
The Funniest People in Relationships: 250 Anecdotes
The Funniest People in Sports: 250 Anecdotes
The Funniest People in Sports, Volume 2: 250 Anecdotes
The Funniest People in Television and Radio: 250 Anecdotes
The Funniest People in Theater: 250 Anecdotes

The Funniest People Who Live Life: 250 Anecdotes
The Funniest People Who Live Life, Volume 2: 250 Anecdotes
The Kindest People Who Do Good Deeds, Volume 1: 250 Anecdotes
The Kindest People Who Do Good Deeds, Volume 2: 250 Anecdotes
Maximum Cool: 250 Anecdotes
The Most Interesting People in Movies: 250 Anecdotes
The Most Interesting People in Politics and History: 250 Anecdotes
The Most Interesting People in Politics and History, Volume 2: 250 Anecdotes
The Most Interesting People in Politics and History, Volume 3: 250 Anecdotes
The Most Interesting People in Religion: 250 Anecdotes
The Most Interesting People in Sports: 250 Anecdotes
The Most Interesting People Who Live Life: 250 Anecdotes
The Most Interesting People Who Live Life, Volume 2: 250 Anecdotes
Reality is Fabulous: 250 Anecdotes and Stories
Resist Psychic Death: 250 Anecdotes
Seize the Day: 250 Anecdotes and Stories

[1] Source: Sandor Katz, *Whoopi Goldberg*, pp. 40-41, 49.

[2] Source: Ann Graham Gaines, *Drew Carey*, p. 72.

[3] Source: Lisa Iannucci, *Ellen DeGeneres: A Biography*, p. 56.

[4] Source: Anne M. Todd, *Chris Rock*, p. 49.

[5] Source: William Donaldson, *Great Disasters of the Stage*, p. 17.

[6] Source: Aaron Hillis, "Filming the Merchant of Venom." *The Village Voice*. 2 October 2007 <http://www.villagevoice.com/film/0740,hillis,77940,20.html>.

[7] Source: Richard Severo, "Joey Bishop, 'Rat Pack' Comic, Dies at 89." *The New York Times*. 19 October 2007 <http://www.nytimes.com/2007/10/19/arts/18cnd-bishop.html?hp>. Also: Michael Freedland, "Obituary: Joey Bishop." *The Guardian*. 24 October 2007 <http://www.guardian.co.uk/obituaries/story/0,,2197717,00.html>.

[8] Source: Greg Dean, *Step by Step to Stand-Up Comedy*, p. 153.

[9] Source: Robert L. Mott, *Radio Live! Television Live!*, p. 109.

[10] Source: Peter Underwood, *Danny La Rue: Life's a Drag!*, p. 66.

[11] Source: Veronica Vera, *Miss Vera's Cross-Dress for Success*, p. 53.

[12] Source: Joey Adams, *The Borscht Belt*, p. 168.

[13] Source: Joan Lowery Nixon, *The Making of a Writer*, pp. 41-46.

[14] Source: Herb Sanford, *Ladies and Gentlemen, The Garry Moore Show: Behind the Scenes When TV was New*, p. 48.

[15] Source: Bill Hicks, *Love All the People*, p. 92.

[16] Source: Morris "Moe" Feinberg, *Larry: The Stooge in the Middle*, p. 117.

[17] Source: H. Allen Smith, *Lost in the Horse Latitudes*, p. 197.

[18] Source: Wally Cox, *My Life as a Small Boy*, pp. 29-33.

[19] Source: Margaret Cho, "When I Think of Tibet." *Huffington Post*. 31 March 2008 <http://www.huffingtonpost.com/margaret-cho/when-i-think-of-tibet_b_94298.html>.

[20] Source: "Hysterical: Google Maps." 30 March 2007 <http://maps.google.com/maps?f=d&hl=en&saddr=chicago,+illinois&daddr=Amsterdam,+Netherlands&layer=&ie=

[21] Source: "My worst ever onstage moment." *The Guardian*. 27 July 2009 <http://www.guardian.co.uk/global/2009/jul/27/comedy-stage>.

[22] Source: Brian Logan, "Any cows in tonight?" *The Guardian*. 14 August 2008 <http://www.guardian.co.uk/stage/2008/aug/14/comedy.edinburghfestival>.

[23] Source: Soupy Sales, *Soupy Sez! My Zany Life and Times*, pp. 67-68.

[24] Source: Peter Underwood, *Danny La Rue: Life's a Drag!*, p. 65.

[25] Source: Gerald Nachman, *Seriously Funny*, p. 14.

[26] Source: Eddie Cantor, *The Way I See It*, p. 76.

[27] Source: Andrea Grimes, "Funny Girl." *The Dallas Observer*. 31 May 2007 <http://www.dallasobserver.com/2007-05-31/news/funny-girl/>.

[28] Source: Hector Gray, *An Actor Looks Back*, p. 22.

[29] Source: Robert Pegg, *Comical Co-Stars of Television*, pp. 17, 21.

[30] Source: Hal Marcovitz, *Robin Williams*, pp. 41, 44-45.

[31] Source: Morris "Moe" Feinberg, *Larry: The Stooge in the Middle*, p. 7.

[32] Source: Margaret Forwood, *The Real Benny Hill*, pp. 76, 81.

[33] Source: Jerry Clower, *Stories from Home*, p. 19.

[34] Source: Groucho Marx, *The Groucho Letters*, p. 55.

[35] Source: Soupy Sales, *Soupy Sez! My Zany Life and Times*, pp. 22, 36.

[36] Source: Michael Shinafelt, "Margaret Cho is 'Beautiful' and So Are Her Gay Fans." 28 January 2008 <http://www.afterelton.com/people/2008/1/margaretcho>.

[37] Source: Andrea Stuart, *Showgirls*, pp. 132-133.

[38] Source: Wally Cox, *My Life as a Small Boy*, pp. 11-15.

[39] Source: Karman Kregloe, "Interview With Liz Feldman." Afterellen.com. 6 April 2008 <http://www.afterellen.com/people/2008/4/lizfeldman>.

[40] Source: Paula Guzzetti, *Jim Carrey*, pp. 14-15, 19-20.

[41] Source: David Hochman, "What George Carlin Told Me About the Afterlife and What He'd Like on His Tombstone." Huffingtonpost.com. 23 June 2008 <http://www.huffingtonpost.com/david-hochman/george-carlin-on-heaven_b_108723.html>.

[42] Source: Frances Lefkowitz, *David Letterman*, pp. 24-26.

[43] Source: Cal and Rose Samra, *Holy Humor*, pp. 84-85.

[44] Source: Bill Zehme, *The Way You Wear Your Hat: Frank Sinatra and the Lost Art of Livin'*, pp. 182-183.

[45] Source: Hal Marcovitz, *Robin Williams*, pp. 21-22, 94.

[46] Source: Tom Mullen, *Seriously, Life is a Laughing Matter*, pp. 26-27.

[47] Source: Don Knotts, *Barney Fife and Other Characters I Have Known*, p. 126.

[48] Source: Michael A. Schuman, *Bill Cosby: Actor and Comedian*, p. 13.

[49] Source: Grace Moore, *You're Only Human Once*, pp. 97-98.

[50] Source: H. Allen Smith, *Lost in the Horse Latitudes*, pp. 193-194.

[51] Source: Greg Dean, *Step by Step to Stand-Up Comedy*, p. 172.

[52] Source: Eddie Cantor and David Freedman, *Ziegfeld: The Great Glorifier*, pp. 66-67.

[53] Source: Chrissy Iley, "Farewell, French and Saunders." 12 August 2007 <http://entertainment.timesonline.co.uk/tol/arts_and_entertainment/ tv_and_radio/article2223828.ece>.

[54] Source: Groucho Marx, *Confessions of a Mangy Lover*, p. 177.

[55] Source: Andrea Stuart, *Showgirls*, pp. 31-32.

[56] Source: Jerry Clower, *Ain't God Good!*, p. 47.

[57] Source: Andrew Hecht, *Hollywood Merry-Go-Round*, p. 30.

[58] Source: S. Claus, *Holiday Cheer for the 19th Hole*, p. 12.

[59] Source: Art Linkletter, *I Didn't Do It Alone*, p. 89.

[60] Source: Jack Mingo, *The Juicy Parts*, p. 114.

[61] Source: Gerald Nachman, *Seriously Funny*, p. 121.

[62] Source: John O'Mahony, "Soap stars." *The Guardian*. 13 February 2008 <http://arts.guardian.co.uk/theatre/drama/story/0,,2255991,00.html>.

[63] Source: Dudley Moore, *Musical Bumps*, p. 144.

[64] Source: Maddy Costa, "I've got a face for comedy." *The Guardian*. 4 September 2007 <http://arts.guardian.co.uk/theatre/comedy/story/ 0,,2161824,00.html>.

[65] Source: Jerry Seinfeld, "Dying Is Hard. Comedy Is Harder." Nytimes.com. 24 June 2008 <http://www.nytimes.com/2008/06/24/opinion/ 24seinfeld.html?_r=1&hp&oref=slogin>.

[66] Source: Roger Ebert: "What's your opinion of the casting, Groucho? 'I haven't fished in years.'" 8 March 1970 <http://rogerebert.suntimes.com/apps/pbcs.dll/article?AID=/19700308/PEOPLE/3080301/1023>.

[67] Source: Tom Feran and R.D. Heldenfels, *Ghoulardi*, pp. 153-154.

[68] Source: Frank Manchel, *Yesterday's Clowns*, p. 77.

[69] Source: Don Knotts, *Barney Fife and Other Characters I Have Known*, pp. 183-184.

[70] Source: Michael A. Schuman, *Bill Cosby: Actor and Comedian*, pp. 98, 108.

[71] Source: Jim Haskins, *Richard Pryor: A Man and His Madness*, p. 11.

[72] Source: Herb Sanford, *Ladies and Gentlemen, The Garry Moore Show: Behind the Scenes When TV was New*, p. 147.

[73] Source: Dick Van Dyke, *Those Funny Kids!*, p. 103.

[74] Source: Rose Blue and Corinne Naden, *Chris Rock*, p. 36.

[75] Source: Sam Levenson, *Everything But Money*, p. 59.

[76] Source: Moe Howard, *Moe Howard and the Three Stooges*, pp. 132-133.

[77] Source: Chaim Topol, compiler, *Topol's Treasury of Jewish Humor, Wit and Wisdom*, p. 123.

[78] Source: Kevin J. Hayes, editor, *Charlie Chaplin: Interviews*, pp. 19-20.

[79] Source: Paula Guzzetti, *Jim Carrey*, pp. 38, 42, 55.

[80] Source: David Morgan, *Monty Python Speaks*, p. 74.

[81] Source: Annie McGarry, *Laurel & Hardy*, p. 76.

[82] Source: Robert Philpot, "Bill Cosby reflects on humor, families and his new book." 28 September 2007 <http://www.popmatters.com/pm/news/article/49122/bill-cosby-reflects-on-humor-families-and-his-new-book/>.

[83] Source: Arnold M. Auerbach, *Funny Men Don't Laugh*, p. 154.

[84] Source: Jim Emerson, "Can Sarah Silverman say that?" 10 November 2005. <http://rogerebert.suntimes.com/apps/pbcs.dll/article?AID=/20051110/EDITOR/51111001>.

[85] Source: Joey Green, *Hi Bob!*, p. 87.

[86] Source: Jim Harmon, *The Great Radio Comedians*, p. 180.

[87] Source: Robert Pegg, *Comical Co-Stars of Television*, p. 68.

[88] Source: Joe Franklin, *Up Late with Joe Franklin*, p. 40.

[89]Source: Joe Garagiola, *It's Anybody's Ballgame*, p. 269.

[90] Source: David Seidman, *Adam Sandler*, p. 12.

[91] Source: StuntDouble, "Lesbian Scientists: The 'Rolling Stone' comedy issue." Afterellen.com. 18 September 2008 <http://www.afterellen.com/blog/stuntdouble/lesbian-scientistics-the-rolling-stone-comedy-issue>. In her blog, StuntDouble included some excerpts from the 2008 *Rolling Stone* comedy issue.

[92] Source: Rose Blue and Corinne Naden, *Chris Rock*, p. 73.

[93] Source: James Bacon, *How Sweet It Is: The Jackie Gleason Story*, pp. 27, 45-46.

[94]Source: Dick DeBartolo, *Good Days and MAD*, p. 52.

[95] Source: Phyllis Diller, *Like a Lampshade in a Whorehouse: My Life in Comedy*, pp. 61-62.

[96] Source: Frank Manchel, *Yesterday's Clowns*, pp. 29-30.

[97]Source: Steve Allen, *But Seriously*, pp. 336-337.

[98]Source: Gordon Irving, compiler, *The Wit of the Scots*, p. 42.

[99] Source: Ta-Nehisi Coates, 'This Is How We Lost to the White Man.' *Atlantic Monthly*. May 2008 <http://www.theatlantic.com/doc/200805/cosby>.

[100]Source: Jim Harmon, *The Great Radio Comedians*, p. xviii.

[101] Source: Barry Dougherty, *A Hundred Years, A Million Laughs*, pp 64-65.

[102] Source: Will Harris, "A Chat with Elliott Gould, Co-star of 'The Caller.'" Bullz-eye.com. 29 April 2009 <http://www.bullz-eye.com/movies/interviews/2009/elliott_gould.htm>.

[103]Source: Joe Garagiola, *It's Anybody's Ballgame*, p. 249.

[104]Source: Groucho Marx, *Confessions of a Mangy Lover*, p. 126.

[105] Source: Danielle Riendeau, "Interview With Jennie McNulty." Afterellen.com. 10 June 2008 <http://www.afterellen.com/people/2008/6/jenniemcnulty>.

[106] Source: Lisa Iannucci, *Ellen DeGeneres: A Biography*, pp. 36-37, 43-44.

[107] Source: Dara Nai, "Five Lesbian Comics You Might Not Know but Should." 17 September 2007 <http://www.afterellen.com/people/2007/9/lesbiancomics>.

[108]Source: Karman Kregloe, "Beaumont Belle: Out Comic Vickie Shaw." 2 May 2006 <http://www.afterellen.com/People/2006/5/vickieshaw2.html>.

[109] Source: Elizabeth Day, "Mr nice guy." *The Observer*. 13 April 2008 <http://arts.guardian.co.uk/theatre/comedy/story/0,,2273165,00.html>.

[110] Source: Kate Clinton, *What the L?*, p. 73.

[111] Source: Bob Smith, "Why I Still Love Gay Pride." 2 July 2006 <http://www.out.com/print_article.asp?id=18898&catid=16>.

[112] Source: Judy Carter, *The Homo Handbook*, p. 131.

[113] Source: Billy Crystal, *700 Sundays*, pp. 155-156.

[114] Source: Larry Kettelkamp, *Bill Cosby: Family Funny Man*, pp. 76, 104-105.

[115] Source: Caroline Tiger, *Margaret Cho*, pp. 29, 31.

[116] Source: Bill Adler and Bruce Cassiday, *The World of Jay Leno: His Humor and His Life*, pp. 182-183.

[117] Source: Hector Gray, *An Actor Looks Back*, p. 6.

[118] Source: Sir Rudolf Bing, *5000 Nights at the Opera*, p. 35.

[119] Source: Billy Crystal, *700 Sundays*, p. 142.

[120] Source: Lila and Rick Guzmán, *George Lopez: Latino King*, pp. 5, 9-12.

[121] Source: Jared Brown, *Zero Mostel: A Biography*, p. 157.

[122] Source: Barry Dougherty, *A Hundred Years, A Million Laughs*, p. 66.

[123] Source: Charles Flowers, editor, *Out, Loud, and Laughing*, p. 118.

[124] Source: Joe Garner, *Made You Laugh*, pp. 76-77. Normally, I would write "n*gger," but in this case, it does not seem appropriate.

[125] Source: Kevin W. Sweeney, editor, *Buster Keaton: Interviews*, pp. 96-97.

[126] Source: David Morgan, *Monty Python Speaks*, p. 294.

[127] Source: Ann Graham Gaines, *Drew Carey*, p. 65.

[128] Source: E. Paul Alworth, *Will Rogers*, pp. 19-20.

[129] Source: Judy Carter, *Stand-Up Comedy: The Book*, p. 150.

[130] Source: Phyllis Diller, *Like a Lampshade in a Whorehouse: My Life in Comedy*, p. 225.

[131] Source: Roger Highfield, "The World's Funniest Joke was Written by Spike Milligan." *The Telegraph*. 15 June 2006 <http://www.telegraph.co.uk/news/main.jhtml?xml=/news/2006/06/09/njoke09.xml>.

[132]Source: Roger Ebert, "Buddy Hackett Never Lost Sight of Importance of Laughter." 2 July 2003 <http://www.suntimes.com/output/eb-feature/cst-ftr-xhack02.html>.

[133] Source: Maxine Marx, *Growing Up with Chico*, p. 30.

[134]Source: Groucho Marx, *The Groucho Letters*, p. 239.

[135]Source: Stan Freberg, *It Only Hurts When I Laugh*, pp. 3-4.

[136]Source: George Burns, *Wisdom of the 90s*, p. 117.

[137]Source: Sir Rudolf Bing, *5000 Nights at the Opera*, pp. 85-86.

[138] Source: Gabe Kaplan, "You'll let me do what?" *The Los Angeles Times*. 4 August 2007 <http://www.latimes.com/news/opinion/commentary/la-oe-kaplan4aug04,0,6491903.story?coll=la-news-comment-opinions>.

[139]Source: Cal and Rose Samra, *Holy Humor*, p. 146.

[140] Source: Richard Grudens, *The Spirit of Bob Hope: One Hundred Years, One Million Laughs*, pp. xiii-xiv. This anecdote comes from Ms. Crosby's "Afterword" to this volume.

[141]Source: Jack Mingo, *The Juicy Parts*, p. 113.

[142]Source: Ed Karvoski, Jr., *A Funny Time to be Gay*, p. 23.

[143] Source: Moe Howard, *Moe Howard and the Three Stooges*, pp. 81, 88, 101.

[144] Source: Richard Grudens, *The Spirit of Bob Hope: One Hundred Years, One Million Laughs*, p. xii. This anecdote comes from Ms. Russell's "Foreword" to this volume.

[145] Source: Kathleen Tracy, *Home Brewed: The Drew Carey Story*, p. 95.

[146] Source: S. Claus, *Holiday Cheer for the 19th Hole*, p. 29.

[147] Source: Dara Nai, "Interview With Rebecca Drysdale." 29 January 2008 <http://www.afterellen.com/people/2008/1/rebeccadrysdale>.

[148]Source: Arnold M. Auerbach, *Funny Men Don't Laugh*, pp. 153-154.

[149] Source: James Bacon, *How Sweet It Is: The Jackie Gleason Story*, pp. xiii-xiv, 75. A C-note is a $100 bill.

[150] Source: Michael Howie, "Last of the music hall legends is still tickled to take centre stage." *The Scotsman*. 2 January 2007 <http://living.scotsman.com/features/Last-of-the-music-hall.3632202.jp>.

[151] Source: Irene Adler, *I Remember Jimmy*, p. 18.

[152]Source: George Burns, *All My Best Friends*, p. 104.

[153] Source: Dominic Maxwell, "French and Saunders on the end of their partnership." *The Times*. 23 September 2008 <http://entertainment.timesonline.co.uk/tol/arts_and_entertainment/stage/comedy/article4803859.ece>.

[154]Source: Andrew Hecht, *Hollywood Merry-Go-Round*, p. 185.

[155]Source: J. Bryan III, *Merry Gentlemen (and One Lady)*, p. 123.

[156]Source: Frances Alda, *Men, Women, and Tenors*, p. 286.

[157] Source: Bill Zehme, *The Way You Wear Your Hat: Frank Sinatra and the Lost Art of Livin'*, p. 14.

[158] Source: Lewis Black, *Me of Little Faith*, p. 45.

[159] David Seidman, *Adam Sandler*, pp. 13-14, 16.

[160] Source: Bernie Mac, *I Ain't Scared of You*, pp. ix-x.

[161] Source: Shauna Swartz, "Meet Judy (aka Jewdy) Gold." 21 November 2006 <http://www.afterellen.com/People/2006/11/judygold.html>.

[162]Source: Cynthia True, *American Scream: The Bill Hicks Story*, p. 89.

[163] Source: Frank Manchel, *The Box Office Clowns*, p. 10.

[164] Source: Kevin W. Sweeney, editor, *Buster Keaton: Interviews*, pp. 42-43, 120-121, 235.

[165] Source: John Anderson, "Ben Stiller: Funny or the heartbreak kid?" 3 October 2007 <http://www.popmatters.com/pm/news/article/49349/ben-stiller-funny-or-the-heartbreak-kid/>.

[166] Source: Joe Franklin, *Up Late with Joe Franklin*, p. 45.

[167]Source: Helen Traubel, *St. Louis Woman*, p. 256.

[168] Source: Jim Haskins, *Richard Pryor: A Man and His Madness*, p. 103.

[169] Source: Steve Johnson, "Steve Martin reunites with his old stand-up partner, the banjo, for serious music." *Chicago Tribune*. 23 October 2009 <http://www.popmatters.com/pm/article/115129-steve-martin-reunites-with-his-old-stand-up-partner-the-banjo-for-se/>.

[170] Source: DustoMcNeato, "Head Over Heels: Literal Video Version." <http://www.youtube.com/watch?v=w0TYun-Nq1Q&NR=1>.

[171]Source: William Claxton, *Laugh*, p. 19.

[172]Source: Dudley Moore, *Musical Bumps*, p. 17.

[173] Source: Kevin J. Hayes, editor, *Charlie Chaplin: Interviews*, p. 49.

[174] Source: Darryl Lyman, *The Jewish Comedy Catalog*, p. 65

[175]Source: Oscar Levant, *A Smattering of Ignorance*, pp. 62-63.

[176] Source: Lewis Black, *Me of Little Faith*, p. 191.

[177]Source: Joey Green, *The Get Smart Handbook*, p. 233.

[178] Source: Sandor Katz, *Whoopi Goldberg*, pp. 19, 22, 36, 64-65.

[179] Source: Lila and Rick Guzmán, *George Lopez: Latino King*, p. 92.

[180]Source: Joey Green, *The Get Smart Handbook*, pp. 5-6.

[181] Source: Joe Garner, *Made You Laugh*, p. 180.

[182]Source: Lawrence J. Epstein, *Mixed Nuts*, p. 220.

[183]Source: Lawrence J. Epstein, *The Haunted Smile*, p. 116.

[184]Source: Cynthia True, *American Scream: The Bill Hicks Story*, p. 47.

[185]Source: Jared Brown, *Zero Mostel: A Biography*, p. 121.

[186]Source: Ron Jenkins, *Acrobats of the Soul*, p. 171. The book Mr. Jillette's quotation comes from was published in 1988, but the joke would be appropriate following the year 2000 Presidential election.

[187] Source: Frank Manchel, *The Box Office Clowns*, p. 9.

[188] Source: Patricia Lopez, "After a lifetime of laughs, Al Franken's on a serious mission." *Star Tribune* (Minneapolis). 23 October 2008 http://www.popmatters.com/pm/article/64792/after-a-lifetime-of-laughs-al-frankens-on-a-serious-mission/.

[189] Source: Ariel Levy, "Don't Laugh." *New York Magazine*. 4 November 2007 <http://nymag.com/news/features/40294/>.

[190] Source: Lewis Black, *Nothing Sacred*, p. 50.

[191] Source: John Eskow, "From Stand-Up Comic to Stand-Up Guy: The Long, Strange Trip of Al Franken." Huffington Post. 7 October 2009 <http://www.huffingtonpost.com/john-eskow/from-stand-up-comic-to-st_b_312047.html>.

[192]Source: Kate Clinton, *What the L?*, pp. 163-164.

[193]Source: Stan Freberg, *It Only Hurts When I Laugh*, p. 30.

[194]Source: Dick DeBartolo, *Good Days and MAD*, pp. 44-45.

[195]Source: Scott Beach, *Musicdotes*, p. 79.

[196] Source: Maxine Marx, *Growing Up with Chico*, pp. 37-38.

[197]Source: Oscar Levant, *A Smattering of Ignorance*, pp. 83-84.

[198] Source: Eddie Cantor and David Freedman, *Ziegfeld: The Great Glorifier*, pp. 138-139.

[199]Source: Frances Alda, *Men, Women, and Tenors*, p. 142.

[200]Source: Steve Allen, *The Funny Men*, p. 262.

[201]Source: George Burns, *All My Best Friends*, p. 189.

[202]Source: J. Bryan III, *Merry Gentlemen (and One Lady)*, p. 274.

[203]Source: Scott Beach, *Musicdotes*, p. 68.

[204]Source: Merrit Malloy and Marsha Rose, *Comedians' Quote Book*, p. 119.

[205]Source: Bill Adler and Bruce Cassiday, *The World of Jay Leno: His Humor and His Life*, p. 4.

[206] Source: Ginny Dougary, "Omid Djalili, seriously funny." *The Times*. 22 March 2008 <http://entertainment.timesonline.co.uk/tol/arts_and_entertainment/stage/comedy/article3590492.ece>.

[207]Source: Lawrence J. Epstein, *The Haunted Smile*, p. 49.

[208]Source: Joey Adams, *The Borscht Belt*, p. 145.

[209] Source: Chris Vognar, "Mocking racism: New wave of humor turns the tables on slurs." *The Dallas Morning News*. 1 February 2008 <http://www.popmatters.com/pm/news/article/53780/mocking-racism-new-wave-of-humor-turns-the-tables-on-slurs/>.

[210] Source: Regina Barreca, editor, *New Perspectives on Women and Comedy*, p. 92.

[211]Source: Brett Butler, *Sold Out*, videotape.

[212]Source: Regina Barreca, editor, *New Perspectives on Women and Comedy*, p. 85.

[213]Source: Bill Hicks, *Love All the People*, pp. 90-91.

[214] Source: Brian Doughtery and the Friars Club, "Introduction" to Soupy Sales' *Stop Me If You're Heard This!*, p. viii.

[215]Source: Tom Feran and R.D. Heldenfels, *Ghoulardi*, pp. 32-33.

[216] Source: Jerry Clower, *Ain't God Good!*, p. 116.

[217] Source: Bill Adler, *Jewish Wit and Wisdom*, pp. 54-55.

[218] Source: Anne M. Todd, *Chris Rock*, p. 21.

[219] Source: Allan Neuwirth, *They'll Never Put That on the Air*, p. 13.

[220] Source: Ron Jenkins, *Acrobats of the Soul*, p. 18.

[221] Source: Larry Kettelkamp, *Bill Cosby: Family Funny Man*, p. 18.

[222] Source: Bernie Mac, *I Ain't Scared of You*, p. 55.

[223] Source: Dick Van Dyke, *Those Funny Kids!*, p. 8.

[224] Source: Keith Elliot Greenberg, *Charles, Burrows, and Charles: TV's Top Producers*, pp. 58-59.

[225] Source: Kathleen Tracy, *Home Brewed: The Drew Carey Story*, pp. 45-46, 50.

[226] Source: Luaine Lee, "Ray Romano hopes everybody loves his new TNT series." McClatchy-Tribune News Service. 1 December 2009 <http://www.popmatters.com/pm/article/117039-ray-romano-hopes-everybody-loves-his-new-tnt-series/>.

[227] Source: Joey Green, *Hi Bob!*, p. 50.

[228] Source: Robert L. Mott, *Radio Live! Television Live!*, p. 107.

[229] Source: Robert Morton, editor, *Stand-up Comedians on Television*, p. 94.

[230] Source: David Kupfer, "In The Jester's Court: Paul Krassner On The Virtues Of Irreverence, Indecency, And Illegal Drugs." *The Sun Magazine*. February 2009, Issue 398 <http://www.thesunmagazine.org/issues/398/in_the_jesters_court>.

[231] Source: Michael Muckian, "The Art (and Science) of Comedy: Martin Short makes them laugh." *Shepherd Express*. 28 May 2008 <http://www.expressmilwaukee.com/article-2279-the-art-(and-science)-of-comedy.html>.

[232] Source: Allan Neuwirth, *They'll Never Put That on the Air*, p. 220.

[233] Source: Bill Adler, *Jewish Wit and Wisdom*, p. 51.

[234] Source: Lewis Black, *Nothing Sacred*, pp. 39, 85.

[235] Source: Caroline Tiger, *Margaret Cho*, p. 36.

[236] Source: William Claxton, *Laugh*, p. 12.

[237] Source: Mark and Ellen Scordato, *The Three Stooges*, p. 57.

[238] Source: Marc Connelly, "Introduction" to Frank Sullivan's *Well, There's No Harm in Laughing*, p. xii.

[239] Source: Darryl Lyman, *The Jewish Comedy Catalog*, p. 146.

[240] Source: Cathy Resmer, "Believe It or Not." *Seven Days*. 29 November 2006 <http://www.sevendaysvt.com/features/2006/believe-it-or-not.html>.

[241] Source: Robert Morton, editor, *Stand-up Comedians on Television*, p. 104.

[242] Source: Frances Lefkowitz, *David Letterman*, pp. 37, 48-49.

[243] Source: Chaim Topol, compiler, *Topol's Treasury of Jewish Humor, Wit and Wisdom*, pp. 41, 55.

[244] Source: Ed Pilkington, "Everybody loves Chris." *The Guardian*. 7 January 2008 <http://film.guardian.co.uk/interview/interviewpages/0,,2236648,00.html>.

[245] Source: Annie McGarry, *Laurel & Hardy*, p. 23.

[246] Source: Kerrie Mills, "Bob & Ray: The Two and Only." 28 March 2008 <http://www.popmatters.com/pm/features/article/55398/bob-ray-the-two-and-only/>.

[247] Source: Mark and Ellen Scordato, *The Three Stooges*, pp. 25-26.

[248] Source: Judy Carter, *Stand-Up Comedy: The Book*, p. 136.

[249] Source: Irene Adler, *I Remember Jimmy*, p. 16.

[250] Source: Shauna Swartz, "Meet Judy (aka Jewdy) Gold." 21 November 2006 <http://www.afterellen.com/People/2006/11/judygold.html>.